To my dear
Daniel
you were

Susan Connolly,

I AM
EDEL

Susan Connolly and Cormac P. Walsh

authorHOUSE®

AuthorHouse™ UK
1663 Liberty Drive
Bloomington, IN 47403 USA
www.authorhouse.co.uk
Phone: UK TFN: 0800 0148641 (Toll Free inside the UK)
        UK Local: (02) 0369 56322 (+44 20 3695 6322 from outside the UK)

Published by AuthorHouse 01/11/2022

ISBN: 978-1-6655-9595-7 (sc)
ISBN: 978-1-6655-9594-0 (e)

Print information available on the last page.

This book is printed on acid-free paper.

CONTENTS

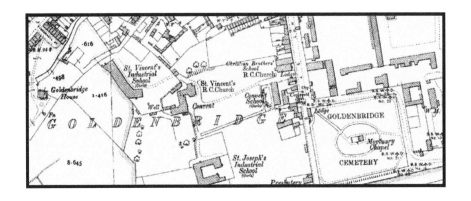

FOREWORD BY EMILIE PINE

Irish society in the 20th Century was scarred by a system of institutions that incarcerated thousands of children and women. These institutions ranged from 'Industrial Schools' for orphans and children taken from their families, to Mother and Child Institutions (commonly known as Mother and Baby Homes) for unmarried mothers, and Magdalen Laundries, for women who were scapegoated for perceived sexual 'sins'. Though they were located in different towns and cities, and run by different religious orders, these institutions had many things in common: they deprived people of their freedom; they fostered emotional, physical and sexual abuse; and they caused – and covered up – the deaths of hundreds of children. Perhaps their most significant and consistent offence was the cruelty with which they treated vulnerable people.

This system of carceral institutions was, for the majority of its operation, protected by an 'iron curtain' of silence. This is not to say that there was no knowledge of the abuses occurring within them, or complaints being made.[1] In fact, we have a long history of individuals brave enough to tell the truth and to challenge the institutions, the State and the Church. It took decades, however, before anyone would listen to the stories of cruelty that emerged from survivors, writers and artists.

I Am Edel joins its voice to that brave chorus and asks us to listen, asks us to see, asks us to understand.

---

[1]   See the analysis of Goldenbridge School (the setting for *I Am Edel*) in the *Report of the Commission to Inquire into Child Abuse* (*CICA*), and the conclusion for example that children in Goldenbridge lived 'in a perpetuate state of fear' (*CICA* Vol II, Chapter 7, par 149) and yet 'The Department of Education inspections observed some problems but missed others. The Inspector did address the issues of food and clothing in the 1940s but … the inspector did not report other, real problems of Goldenbridge, including the excessive chores, the pressures of bead making and the emotional deprivation. These problems could have been discovered by speaking to the children.' (*CICA* Vol II, Chapter 7, General Conclusion 11). For a discussion of the Industrial School system see Mary Raftery and Eoin O'Sullivan, *Suffer the Little Children: The Inside Story of Ireland's Industrial Schools* (New York: Continuum, 1996); see also Emilie Pine, *The Politics of Irish Memory* (Basingstoke: Palgrave, 2010), pp.20-25.

A history of speaking out

In the 1960s, Richard Johnson's play, *The Evidence I Shall Give*, brought to public attention the cruelty of nuns towards their charges in an orphanage managed by an order of Catholic nuns. Running for a remarkable eighty-seven performances in 1961, the play presents the story of Margaret Rafferty, a young girl who has been repeatedly punished for the offence of trying to comfort her younger siblings, and also attempting to run away to bring them back home to their father (the children were not orphans, but were institutionalised following the death of their mother). The final punishment of Margaret occurs after her attempt to run away, when Sister Mary brutally cuts the girl's hair. The revelation of this disfiguring punishment in the play's courtroom set, causes the other characters to gasp in outrage. Johnson was encouraged by the Abbey's Director to create a 'happy ending', and so the play ends with Margaret forgiving Sister Mary. Nevertheless, the routine vindictiveness of the treatment of vulnerable and grieving children had been revealed by the play. As the Ryan Report testifies, the play's successful long-run is an 'indicator' that there was an audience open to hearing stories of abuse, yet despite this it failed to translate into any action outside the theatre.[2]

Published memoirs and novels were other outlets for former child-residents of Industrial Schools to make public the abuses they suffered. In 1983, Mannix Flynn published his first autobiographical novel, *Nothing to Say*, and in 1988 Paddy Doyle published the non-fiction *The God Squad*, both books detailing the cruelty of life in the institutions, and the long-term consequences of the abuse they both suffered. Flynn would go on to make many cultural works, including the play *James X* (2003), a play that again used the material of his life and incarceration in Letterfrack Boys School, to expose the abuse of children by the Catholic religious orders tasked with their care.

It was not until the 1990s, however, that these kinds of stories gained mainstream traction. In 1996, Louis Lentin's documentary *Dear Daughter* about St. Vincent's Industrial School, Goldenbridge was screened by RTÉ, Ireland's national broadcaster. This documentary includes harrowing

---

[2]   *Report of the Commission to Inquire into Child Abuse* Vol 4, chapter 1, par 169-173.

first-person testimony, led by Christine Buckley who narrates her experiences direct to camera, captured in a close-up that is not only emotionally affecting but creates absolute credibility. Following the documentary's screening, it seemed, audiences were ready not only to listen, but to talk. Radio phone-in shows became a space for people to share their own experiences as the stigma associated with the institutions began to shift away from the blameless children who had been incarcerated and onto the religious orders who managed the institutions and were responsible for so much of the abuse. Susan Connolly herself was affected by seeing *Dear Daughter* and began to find ways to tell her own story, a journey which has led to this extraordinary play.

Three years after *Dear Daughter*, RTÉ broadcast *States of Fear*, a three-part documentary by the investigative journalist Mary Raftery, which exposed the abuses that had occurred across many of the Industrial Schools. The programmes had a dramatic impact on the public, sparking widespread outrage, and leading directly to the government's official apology, delivered on 11 May 1999, just hours before the broadcast of the final episode. Delivered by then-Taoiseach Bertie Ahern, the government apologised to thousands of 'victims of childhood abuse' in the institutions.[3] Subsequently, the government founded a Commission of Investigation, which published a report in 2009, officially endorsing what survivors had said for decades: that the Industrial Schools for Ireland's vulnerable children were a system of abuse.

Ireland's history of institutionalisation is no longer a silenced narrative. Yet there are so many stories remaining to be told, to be heard, and acknowledged.

I Am Edel

In *I Am Edel*, Susan Connolly and Cormac Plunkett Walsh evoke the story of one young girl who finds herself suddenly institutionalised in Goldenbridge. Entering the industrial school, the girl leaves behind the world she knows – her clothes are taken, her hair is cut, even her name is taken when she is renamed 'number 2'. It is a harsh world that she

---

3   Bertie Ahern, Apology, 11 May 1999. Watch online: https://www.rte.ie/archives/2019/0430/1046590-apology-to-victims-of-institutional-child-abuse/

joins – there's never enough food, the children are forced to make rosary beads, she is separated from her brothers, and undergoes constant verbal and physical abuse.

But while Edel suffers from these cruelties, something in her spirit refuses to be bowed. She forms friendships, acts out imaginary scenes, and finds consolation in knowing who she really is. Edel's undimmed appetite for life and her resilience are some of the aspects of *I Am Edel* that makes this play such an important contribution to the body of creative work representing Ireland's institutional past. Children have the most wonderful capacity for joy and play, even in the worst of circumstances and under the most terrible oppression. When Edel and her friends yell 'Geronimo', when they escape from the institution, when they sing songs, or express care for each other the audience gets to witness not only their pain but also their natural strength and beauty. Too often survivors of institutional abuse are represented in one-dimensional ways, defined only by their suffering. Not so in this play.

Sharing her memories and fictionalising them for this play cannot have been easy for Susan Connolly. That she has taken the risk of doing so is a testament to the healing work she has committed to over the past decades, and her own inner strength, belief in herself, and recognition of the necessity for these stories to be heard. It is also a testament to the supportive context of the Christine Buckley Education and Support Centre and their drama group, led by Cormac Plunkett Walsh.

In *I Am Edel*, Connolly and Walsh allow audiences to enter into the world of the children. In conveying this painful past, Connolly and Walsh give us insight into what it feels like to be plunged into despair, and how it can be survived. This is a lesson in Irish history. A lesson in individual survival. A lesson in why we need to guard against such institutionalisation ever happening again.

And it is a lesson on all the ways that children need and deserve love and care, not cruelty.

Emilie Pine is Professor of Modern Drama at University College Dublin, and is author of the No.1 non-fiction bestseller Notes to Self.

SETTING AND CHARACTERS

The play is entitled *I am Edel*. It refers to the protagonists Confirmation name. In writing this play we decided to use the name Edel (as script line name) from the start of the play although the eponymous character is in some scenes referred to as Number Two or Siobhan, and only as Edel in the scene *Edel and Big Brown Box* and thereafter.

Notes on staging

The Play is set in Sisters of Mercy, St Vincent's Industrial School, Goldenbridge, Dublin.

The set consists of several staging areas. These are:

- A workroom for rosary bead making and laundry.
- A scullery with a door to the outside and a hatch to the corridor.
- A central corridor.
- Dormitory with metal frame beds and curtained partitions.
- A large central stairwell.
- An office.
- A secret attic.
- A toilet with cisterns with long chains.
- The Visitors Room
- All windows are barred.

Religious statues are ubiquitous throughout the set.

During each core scene different parts of the staging areas are active with muted phatic dialogue.

CHARACTERS

Orphans
Edel
Anne
Mary J
Moira
Marian
Maggy
Bernadette
Maire
Mary L
Geraldine
Boy one (*Mícheál*)
Boy two (*Dáithí*)
*Nicola has a notable speech impediment.

Nuns
Sister Etrusca Lisieux
Sister Claudine

Other Characters
Orla Murphy
The Lady and The Man

Lay People
Nicola*
Fat & Slimy Mary
Mrs. Rilley

LIST OF SCENES

Each scene has its own title. These intertitles are projected.

Act one

1. The Beginning
2. How to Make Rosary Beads
3. Three Children of Fatima
4. I Could be Geronimo
5. The Bread Winner
6. Thank You
7. Mr. Patchy Britches
8. Hong Kong
9. Blank Canvas
10. Dust Tea Party

Act Two

1. Mizing
2. Seven Days in the Scullery
3. The Murder Monologues
4. Edel and the Big Brown Box
5. Dr Dolittle
6. Assumptive On Me Birthday
7. Dead Fish
8. The End

ACT ONE

SCENE 1

The Beginning

*Intertitle: **The Beginning***

Sister Etrusca Lisieux: Nicola! Bring them in.

Lights fade up.

Two nuns are seated at a desk in the visitors' room. They are looking at a role book. Two Lay People, Nicola and Fat N' Slimy Mary, are standing with arms folded beside the desk.

Three small children enter, a girl aged five with two boys aged four and three. They are dressed neatly and are clutching small suitcases. The girl has long, braided red hair.

Sister Claudine: Now look at you.

Sister Etrusca Lisieux: All the way from England.

Sister Claudine: Bexhill-on-Sea. They are very neat.

Sister Etrusca Lisieux: They won't fit in.

Sister Claudine: Look at her hair.

Sister Etrusca Lisieux: Oh dear. That'll have to go, child.

Sister Claudine: And the boys?

Sister Etrusca Lisieux: They'll most likely have nits. They're easy enough. Have them shaved.

Sister Claudine: Right, children, put your little suitcases over there. You won't be needing them here.

The children place the suitcases by the desk. Nicola smirks. One of the boys starts shivering.

Sister Claudine: Oh, he's obviously a bed-wetter. Mary, he can be placed in the Wet-the-Bed Dormitory. The other boy can go down to the prefabs. Now the girl.

Fat N Slimy Mary: There's a spare bed in St Bernadette's Dormitory, Sister.

Nicola and Fat N' Slimy Mary exchange a conspiratorial glance.

Sister Etrusca Lisieux: So we need some clothes that will fit in here. So, children, remove those clothes.

Edel: But—but—I got this dress for my birthday.

Sister Claudine: Ha ha! We don't do birthdays here, child.

Edel: But I got this from the other nuns in England.

Sister Etrusca Lisieux whacks the desk with a stick.

Sister Etrusca Lisieux: We are not in England. This is Ireland.

Pause.

Sister Etrusca Lisieux: Nicola, take their clothes.

The children are stripped to their underwear.

Sister Etrusca Lisieux: What's your name?

Edel: *[Coughs softly]* Siobhan. My name's Siobhan, and these are my little brothers—

Sister Claudine: Huh. That is quite the accent you have.

Sister Etrusca Lisieux: Indeed. And the hair is too long. Mary!

Fat & Slimy Mary stands to attention.

Sister Etrusca Lisieux: Get the scissors. Girl, you stand on this chair.

Sister Etrusca Lisieux pulls the chair out beside the desk. Edel stands on the chair.

Sister Etrusca Lisieux: Nicola, shave the boys.

Nicola eagerly brings the boys to the far side of the desk and commences shaving their heads.

Two slightly older children enter. They stare at Edel.

Sister Claudine: Numbers Twenty-Three and Thirty-Eight, just wait *[she writes in the ledger]*. Get started on the new quota of rosary beads in St Philomena's.

Exit the older children.

Sister Etrusca Lisieux: Now you three need numbers. These numbers will be on all items of clothing until you are sixteen years of age and leave this establishment.

Sister Claudine: Well, this one is girl number two this year.

Sister Etrusca Lisieux: You are Number Two.

She cuts Edel's braid.

Sister Etrusca Lisieux: You can keep this if you wish.

3

Edel holds her braid tightly.

Sister Etrusca Lisieux: Bells go off for Morning Call, Benediction, Mass, breakfast, and dinner. Get used to it. Go with Mary now to the workroom to get your new clothes.

Blackout.

ACT ONE

SCENE 2

How to Make Rosary Beads

Intertitle: **How to Make Rosary Beads**

Sound of a metronome.

Dark stage, then lights slowly fade up on a row of vintage school desks. There are no pens beside the inkwells. Children seated at desks are gradually illuminated in silhouette. The seated children's hands emerge from the darkness. They raise the desk covers. Methodically they gather objects from the raised desk. They close the desk cover and place three objects on the cover. The objects are wires, pliers, and beads.

Enter Fat N' Slimy Mary, shoving Edel into the room.

Fat N' Slimy Mary: Four! Five! Make room, push over there. We've got a newbie. This is Number Two. Sit there, Number Two.

Edel sits between Mary J and Mary L.

Fat N' Slimy Mary: Go on. We haven't got all day. Get yourself a pliers.

Mary J: Here take this. It's my old one.

Edel looks very nervous.

Mary L: Don't cry—they'll all just pick on you.

Anne: Number Two. Come over here, sit beside me.

Edel approaches.

Anne: I am the best at this. Here, this is what you do. I'll show you how to string the wire. Here, just get the beads. Just string them along the wire. Just like this. Put a loop like this at the other end so the beads won't fall off. Yeah. That's how you do it. That's good. You are a fast learner.

Edel: Thanks. Thanks for showing me.

Anne: You talk funny.

Edel: That's what the nuns said, that I had an … *accent.*

Anne: An accident?

Edel: Yeah, it's an English one.

Mary J: We'll knock that out of ye.

Mary L: We'll get you talking Goldenbridge.

Anne: What's yer name?

Edel: Siobhan. Siobhan Mary. What's yours?

Anne: Anne. Anne Myfanwy. Myfanwy. It's Welsh.

Bernadette: It sounds like fanny. Is your mother a fallen woman?

Edel: I think so. That's what the nun said.

Anne: My mammy's fallen too.

Mary L: And mine.

Mary J: Mine too!

Anne: That's why we have to make holy rosary beads.

Bernadette: Jaysus, Siobhan, you're really good at making them. Look at that, girls.

Mary J: They'll keep you.

Fade.

Fade up.

A nun in silhouette paces slowly in the foreground between the children and their desks. The nun is swirling a large bunch of rosary beads. They are noisy as the nun paces.

The children are slowly illuminated. They are tired. They are making rosary beads. They are counting like slaves in a Roman galley ship.

Children: One. Two. Three. Four. Five. Six. Seven. Eight …

A bell rings in the distance. The children and the nun stop simultaneously. It is a distant bell. The children have all reached to their left. The nun turns.

Nun: That's not our bell. Eight!

Children: Nine. Ten.

A bell rings closely. The children all snatch a rosary bead from their left. The nun turns.

Nun: That's our bell. Now children, let us pray.

Nun *and* **Children:** My Lord God, even now I accept at Thy hands, cheerfully and willingly, with all its anxieties, pains and sufferings, whatever kind of death it shall please Thee to be mine. Amen.

The children continue working.

Children: One. Two. Three. Four. Five. Six. Seven. Eight. Nine. Ten. One. Two. Three. Four. Five. Six. Seven. Eight. Nine. Ten.

They repeat the count until a bell rings closely. The children all snatch a rosary bead from their right. The nun exits. The children continue working. Child One surreptitiously stares eating a bit of bread.

Anne: I wish we could do something different.

Edel: What do you want to be when you grow up?

Bernadette: I want to be a warrior!

Mary J: I want to be a fireman and burn this effing place down!

Anne, Edel, Bernadette, Mary J: Yeah!

Mary L: I want to be a nun!

The children suddenly fall silent, all looking at Mary L. The sound of a metronome continues. The nun slowly paces across the stage. The sound of her rosary beads recedes as she walks off.

Mary L: A good one.

Mary J: How could you be a nun with your gammy leg?

Edel stands with arms raised solemnly.

Edel: "Give us this day our daily bread." An effing nun, for God sake, Mary L!

Anne: God didn't say throw the bread out the window.

Bernadette: Mouldy rubbish.

The nun enters.

Nun: Cunas!

The children are making rosary beads.

Fade.

ACT ONE

SCENE 3

Three Children of Fatima

Intertitle: ***Three Children of Fatima***

All children are outside playing in the field. It is a bright sunny day. Edel is building an imaginary house out of freshly cut grass. She is very involved with this world. Mícheál and Dáithí are playing Cowboys and Indians. They are chasing each other.

Edel: I am the queen, and this ... this is my palace.

Mícheál and Dáithí charge into the Grass Palace, destroying it.

Edel: Ye bleedin' eejits! Look what ye did to me palace!

Edel attacks the boys. Mrs Rilley, a lay person, extricates Edel from the melee.

Mrs Rilley: You little brat. Do not be picking on your little brothers!

Edel: They started it, Miss!

Mrs Rilley: They did not. I saw what I saw. I am taking you to the sister's office, so I am. And you two boys. Yes you! Get back to the yard!

Mrs Rilley locks Edel in a half nelson and shoves her towards the office and sits her down.

Mrs Rilley: I'm getting Sister Etrusca Lisieux. You'll be making rosary beads for the rest of the day, so you will.

Mrs Rilley exits.

9

Edel looks around. She slowly stands. The office is daunting. It is filled with crosses and religious images of the Blessed Virgin and the Sacred Heart. These are highlighted by a follow spot.

She slowly approaches the desk. On it are rosary beads, prayer books, Bibles, and a punishment stick. She slowly lifts the punishment stick. She quickly lays it back on the table. She returns to the seat and sits.

Edel stands. She very cautiously approaches the desk. She sits in the nun's chair. Her Brothers appear in the office window making faces. Edel doesn't see them. She gets up. Slowly and deliberately she clasps the punishment stick in her right hand. She raises it above her head. She violently whacks the desk. At the window her brothers gasp/exclaim loudly.

Edel: *[Speaks in a loud whisper]* What are yiz doing here?

Behind the boys Mrs Rilley suddenly appears.

Mrs Rilley: Right now the three of yous are in trouble. Stand over there. Look at yous.

Exit Mrs. Rilley.

The boys are highly upset. Edel puts her arm around their shoulders. She too is scared but is determined not to show it.

Mícheál: What's going to happen to us?

Dáithí: I wanna go back out and play.

Enter Sister Etrusca Lisieux.

Sister Etrusca Lisieux: What are you doing here in my office?

Edel: Mrs Rilley said you've to punish us, Sister.

Sister Etrusca Lisieux: What sort of punishment should you receive?

Pause.

Sister Etrusca Lisieux: Speak up, child. Has the cat got your tongue?

Edel nervously touches her tongue with her left hand while hiding her right hand behind her back.

Edel: No, sister.

Sister Etrusca Lisieux: Hmmmm. What would please God?

Pause. She goes to the desk and slowly moves the punishment stick across the desk.

Hmmmm?

Pause.

Sister Etrusca Lisieux: A dozen rosary beads would please the lord. Wouldn't it?

Edel, Mícheál, Dáithí: Yes Sister Etrusca Lisieux.

Sister Etrusca Lisieux opens a drawer in the desk and retrieves three objects which she places on the desk.

Sister Etrusca Lisieux: Beads, pliers, wires. Now. Twelve. One dozen.

Exit Sister Etrusca Lisieux.

Edel: Boys shush! Don't be afraid … Did you hear about the Three Children of Fatima?

Mícheál: Didn't they see our Lady?

Dáithí: She was lovely, so she was.

Edel: Do you know what? We look like the Three Children of Fatima. Look why don't we just get the angels to make the rosary beads

Dáithí: Jesus! Angels!

Mícheál: How are you going to make them do that?

Edel: Look we'll go into the dark corridor over there.

The three children flit into the semi darkness.

Edel: Now we'll call the angels. And while we're here the angels will make the rosary beads in there.

Edel adopts a religious pose.

Nothing happens.

The boys start sobbing

Edel: Boys, don't be scared. Like, they're not going to hurt us. They'll be in the other room making the rosary beads.

Mícheál and **Dáithí:** Our father artist in heaven, hello be thy name, dye kingdom done, I will be - Jaysus!

The office door starts to open very slowly. A tall dark figure appears silhouetted in the doorway. The three children scream.

Sister Etrusca Lisieux: What are you doing here?

Edel: Sister Etrusca Lisieux! We were just praying to ... to... to ...we are the Three Children of Fatima, and we were just praying to the Angels to make the Rosary beads so we could go back out and play.

Sister Etrusca Lisieux: Oh for goodness sake get out and play.

Blessing themselves the children dash through the door. Mrs Rilley is in the yard.

Mrs Rilley: What are you doing outside?

Edel: The angels are making the rosary beads. It's a miracle.

Sister Etrusca Lisieux: I told them to go out and play Mrs Rilley.

Blackout. Sound of children playing happily.

ACT ONE

SCENE 4

I Could Be Geronimo

Intertitle: ***I Could Be Geronimo***

Anne and Edel are seated a desk making rosary beads. A nun approaches.

Sister Etrusca Lisieux: How are we getting on girls?

Anne and Edel: We are doing God's work Sister Etrusca Lisieux.

Sister Etrusca Lisieux: God bless the work. Sixty a day and ninety on Saturday. And you two girls find yourselves all alone on a Sunday having to make another forty sets of beads.

Anne and Edel: We were bold Sister Etrusca Lisieux.

Sister Etrusca Lisieux: You were.

Anne and Edel: We won't be bold again Sister Etrusca Lisieux.

Sister Etrusca Lisieux: And pigs will fly.

Pause.

Sister Etrusca Lisieux: Carry on.

Anne and Edel: Thank you Sister Etrusca Lisieux.

Exit Sister Etrusca Lisieux.

Pause.

Anne: Why do nuns have such effing weird names?

Edel: Shush!

Pause.

The girls continue their labour.

Edel slowly looks around.

Edel: It's because they were never children.

Anne: That's mad. Of course they were children. They had Mammys and Daddies.

Edel: How do you know?

Anne: Well they definitely would have had the Lady and the Man.

Pause … The girls are silently whispering numbers as they make rosary beads.

Edel: Did you ever hear of a nun called Amy, or Sharon or Geraldine? Seriously would a Man or a Lady name you Deciduous?

Anne: Deciduous?

Edel: After Sister Deciduous.

Anne: Deciduous? What kind of name is that?

Edel: It's a type of tree. It grows rhubarbs.

Pause … The two girls methodically continue their labour.

Anne: I'd call meself Sister Bacteria Cafeteria!

Edel: I'd never call meself after an effing nun. Walking down dusty corridors swinging me effing rosary beads terrorising poor little brats.

Flinging mouldy bread for them to chase. Feck that I'd be different. I'd be ... id be ... I'd ...

Edel jumps up. Pause ... Her beads settle on the desk.

Anne: So what would you be?

Pause ... Edel flops back to her seat. She resumes making rosary beads.

Anne: I had a Sister Constantinople once. I could never pronounce her name, but she bet it into me. Not as bad as Maggie Four she called her Sister Constipated the Miracle of Flattula. She broke Maggie Four's arm. That was funny.

Pause ... Edel sits up.

Anne: In a bad way.

Pause.

Anne: Or maybe I would be sister Contrapta. Maker of a contraption that would make effing rosary beads without children.

Pause.

Anne: Are you alright?

Pause.

Edel suddenly stands defiantly with one arm aloft.

Edel: I could be Geronimo!

Anne: Who's Geronimo?

Edel: I'm Geronimo! Listen ... Shush!

Pause.

Edel: It's the Wild West. Buffalos and deserts and canyons and choo-choo trains – can you hear the whistle:

Anne and Edel: Choo-Choo! Choo-Choo! Chug, chug, chug, chug!

Anne and Edel imitate the wheels of a steam train.

Edel: Bright sunshine everywhere. Cowboys and Injuns. Look at my War bonnet. See my fine feathers of yellow, purple and green. Multi-coloured fantastical! All woven in with the red, gold and green beads I won from General Birds Eye Custard.

She mimics firing a bow and arrow.

There I was at the Battle of the Little Big Yer Wan. Another feather in my extremely brilliant cap.

Anne: You don't have anything on yer head.

Edel: Would you use your imagination! Look –

Edel jumps onto the chair.

There's dastardly Yankees on one side even more dastardly Mexicans to the other. I have me spear-

Anne: Where did you learn about all of this?

Edel: The Lady and the Man had a telly.

Anne: Uuuuuuuhhhh! They sound like a great Lady and Man.

Pause

Edel: The best.

Anne: They had a colourdy telly? Wow!

17

Edel: A colourdy telly?

Pause.

Edel: No it was in black and white, so it was.

Anne: So how did you know what colours Geronimo's feathers and beads were then?

Edel is unimpressed.

Edel: I … used … my … imagicnation! Look at me I'm getting ready for battle. For the fight!

Edel jumps onto the desk.

Edel: I call my Apache braves! The battle cry is Geronimo! Geronimo! Come on you-

Anne jumps up and stands defiantly.

Anne and Edel: Geronimo! Geronimo! Geronimo!!!

Edel: I put me war paint on! My beautiful skin is tanned by the Wild West sun.

Anne: Yer not starkers are ye!?

Edel: Of course not … I have a loin cloth for to cover me bits … I have my war spear. I wave it above my head. All my Apache braves mount their fine brown horses. My Beautiful white horse is ready. We are ready for the Fight. The Mexicans are too scared to fight! They run away! The Yankees look scared!

Anne: We will fight them on the beaches!

Edel jumps on Anne's back.

Edel: Geronimo! Ye ha! Giddy up. Charge! Charge! Charge!

Anne and Edel: Charge! Charge! Charge!

Anne runs around in circles with Edel piggy backing.

Edel: Geronimo! I've got my bow and arrow. There's a lay person! I shoot a lay person! Hooray!

Anne and Edel: Geronimo! Geronimo! Geronimo!!!

Edel: I shoot another one. And another one there. I am on fire! I am Geronimo!

Anne: Kill them! Kill them! Kill them all!

Anne and Edel: Charge! Charge! Charge!

Sister Etrusca Lisieux appears upstage. She is purposefully twirling an oversized set of Rosary Beads.

Edel: And I get another arrow and I shoot a nun! Geronimo leads the Apaches out of Goldenbridge!

Sister Etrusca Lisieux: You heinous little brat!

Sister Etrusca Lisieux swings the Rosary Beads and bludgeons Edel in the face. Edel falls from Anne's back onto the floor. She is bleeding and sobbing in a very shocked state. Anne falls to the floor cowering.

Pause.

Sister Etrusca Lisieux is in a state of panic.

Sister Etrusca Lisieux: Stop your wretched whinging! Stop it I say! Look what you've done. There's blood on the floor. Clean it up now. Scrub that floor! You are a show.

Blackout.

ACT ONE

SCENE 5

The Breadwinner

*Intertitle: **The Breadwinner***

The kids are in the school yard. They are playing Hopscotch and other games. All of them are keeping an eye on a sash window that overlooks the courtyard. Edel is repeatedly climbing on a low wall and jumping off, flapping her arms.

Anne: What are you doing?

Edel: I'm flying.

Anne: Yeah, and my daddy's King of the Army.

Edel: That's rubbish. Would you help me here, I am actually doing the early preparation for flying. Look I climb up on the wall. I close my eyes and I think like a bird.

Anne: How do you think like a bird?

Edel: Shush! Would you bleeding contemplate?

Anne: How do ye … count … dem … plates?

Edel: You think like a bird and jump.

Edel starts flapping her arms gently. She takes a deep breath and jumps frantically waving her arms. She lands on her feet, turns and climbs back on the wall.

Edel: That … is … how … you … fly.

The sash window opens across the courtyard. A bell rings. All the children scream. "Scraps!"

All the children scramble to get as near to the window as possible. A big tin basin filled with chunks of bread from uncut loaves appears.

Nicola pretends to throw the bread. Teasing and confusing the kids. She throws a few bits and then ultimately empties the entire bin.

Nicola: Reef them out of it!

Edel catches sight of a buttered corner of bread. Marie sees it at the same time. They both miss it in midair. Marie grabs the bread on the ground. Edel stamps on her hand grinding it into the ground. Marie runs off screaming.

Edel strolls through the crowded courtyard sits on the low wall beside Anne and eats her bread contentedly.

Edel: This bread is gorgeous.

Anne: It's got butter.

Edel: And there's hardly any mold.

Anne: Look at the crust on that.

Edel mizes the bread and licks the butter. At the far side of the yard a nun and layperson usher Marie away. Marie is crying uncontrollably.

Blackout

ACT ONE

SCENE 6

Thank You

*Intertitle: **Thank You***

Children are in the dormitory. It looks like a hospital ward. Edel rushes in. She pulls the curtain closed. She is panicky and uncertain. She lies on her bed pretending to be asleep.

[Off] **Marie:** Where is she? Where is she? Where's Siobhan?

Bernadette: Marie's back from the hospital.

Anne: You're in trouble now.

Mary J: She'll batter ye.

Edel: In the jame of naysus!

Bernadette: What are you going to do?

Anne: She's coming for ye.

Anne and **Bernadette:** *[Sing]* "She's coming for ye/ She's coming for ye."

Mary J: She'll batter ye.

Edel: Jesus, Mary and shite!

[Off] **Marie:** Where is she?

Marie swishes open the curtain.

22

Marie: Where is she? There you are! Wait till I tell you what happened. You're never gonna give a guess, right, me fingers are broken. Look.

Marie raises her hand. Three of her fingers are in metal splints.

Edel: I'm really sorry, I, I -

Marie: Yeah but their really broken. Look. Look what they had to do. They had to put these three splints on them. Guess what.

All: What?

Pause.

Marie: I loved it. The nurses took great care of me. It was brilliant. I loved been in hospital. They X rayed me.

Mary J: What's that?

Marie: *[Speaks slowly]* It's a yoke that sees through you and takes pictures of yer bones.

Bernadette: That's bleeding amazing.

Marie: O I love it. They put these metal things on me fingers. Look. Look at that.

Anne: You're like a robot.

Marie: I won't be able to make rosary beads.

All: Wow!

Marie: I wont be able to make rosary beads. I have got not one, not two but three broken fingers and I … wont … be … able … to … Make rosary beads!

All gasp in amazement.

23

Mary J: For how long?

Marie: Probably for never.

Marie makes as if to hug Edel. Edel recoils.

Marie: Oh you'd love hospital. You'd love it! They take great care of you there and the food's brilliant, so it is and they give you sweets and jelly and ice cream. Aw thanks you're a star.

Marie hugs Edel.

Edel: Thanks Marie.

Marie: Ah thank you, thank you, thank you!

Pause.

Marie: I love you for what you did for me.

A bell rings. The children get into their beds.

Blackout

Moira: Siobhan. Will you break my arm?

Anne: And mine?

ACT ONE

SCENE 7

Mr. Patchy Britches

Intertitle: **Mr. Patchy Britches**

The Schoolyard.

The Children are playing. Edel, Anne and Bernadette are humming a tune.

Edel: Ok you got the tune. And now the words. *[Sings]* "Little Mr. Patchy Britches"

Anne *and* **Bernadette:** "Little Mr. Patchy Britches"

Edel, Anne *and* **Bernadette:** "Little Mr. Patchy Britches"

Edel: Again.

Edel, Anne *and* **Bernadette:** "Little Mr. Patchy Britches"

Upstage Mary J, Moira and Mary L are playing with a tennis ball. They are playing Piggy-in-the-middle. Mary L who has polio, is in the middle.

Edel: Now. I'm going to add the next bit. So it goes "Little Mr. Patchy Britches. I Love you"

Bernadette: People will give us money for this?

Edel: Loads. Now shush! "Little Mr. Patchy Britches, I Love you"

Edel, Anne *and* **Bernadette:** "Little Mr. Patchy Britches, I Love you"

Edel: Brilliant! Again.

Edel, Anne *and* **Bernadette:** "Little Mr. Patchy Britches, I Love you"

Edel: yeah, yeah!

Edel, Anne *and* **Bernadette:** "Little Mr. Patchy Britches, I Love you"

The tennis ball bounces past the three singers. Mary L limps after it and picks it up. She observes the singers and bounces the ball.

Edel: "If you'll be my Sunday fellow"

Edel, Anne *and* **Bernadette:** "If you'll be my Sunday fellow"

Edel: From the beginning.

Edel, Anne *and* **Bernadette:** "Little Mr. Patchy Britches, I Love you/ If you'll be my Sunday fellow"

Pause.

Bernadette: Jaysus! That was great!

Edel: People are going to give us lots of money!

Anne: Ballyfermot here we come!

Mary L throws the ball over the singers

Mary L: Moira! Catch it!

The tennis ball hits Moira. She and Mary J fight over it. Mary L sits beside the singers. She takes off and examines her plastic shoes.

Edel: And the next lines go "I'll patch you in pink and in green and in yellow/ And all day long/ We'll be singing our happy song."

Edel, Anne *and* **Bernadette:** "I'll patch you in pink and in green and in yellow/ And all day long/ We'll be singing our happy song."

The singers cheer.

Mary L : What are youz at?

Pause.

Mary L: That's a lovely song.

Pause.

Mary L: I can sing. My Lady and Man said so. So. Can I join yez?

Bernadette: Can you sing in front of people?

Mary L: I could sing in front of the whole wide world.

Bernadette: Brilliant! Edel can she come with us?

Edel and Anne stare at Bernadette.

Mary L: *[Sings badly]* "If you'll be my Sunday Fellow/ I'll give you marshmallows of pink and of yellow"

Edel, Anne and Bernadette all laugh.

Bernadette: She'll make them laugh.

Mary L: Who?

Edel, Anne *and* **Bernadette:** The outsiders!

Edel gasps.

Mary L: Youz are gonna run away.

Bernadette: Shush!

Anne: *[Whispers aggressively]* You keep your voice down!

27

Mary: *[Speaks in singsong]* Youz are running away.

Pause.

Anne: I told you to shut up.

Mary L: I won't say anything if you take me with you.

Anne: We're not taking you. You've got a gammy leg.

Mary L: You shut yer face!

Edel: Wait!

Pause.

Edel: She's coming with us.

All four girls join hands.

Edel, Anne, Bernadette *and* **Mary L:** Cross me heart, don't tell a lie or else the four of us will surely die.

The tea bell rings. The girls skip out of the yard singing.

Edel, Anne, Bernadette *and* **Mary L:** "I'll patch you in pink and in green and in yellow/ And all day long/ We'll be singing our happy song."

Fade.

Edel: Shush! It's our secret.

ACT ONE

SCENE 8

Hong Kong

Intertitle: **Hong Kong**

Traditional Irish music is playing [off].

There is a clock that reads Six Forty-Five.

Mary J is 'mizing' bread. She is sitting on the ground underneath the scraps window. Marie is sitting in another part of the yard. She looks at her hand. Cloth bandages loosely adorn three of her fingers. She undoes the bandages and starts retying them.

Mary J finishes her bread. She goes to Marie.

Mary J: You're not fooling anybody.

Marie: Jaysus!

Mary J: Do you want me to give you a hand?

Marie: Yeah. This is messy.

Mary J: "Give you a hand." See what I did there? See what I did there ye big eejit.

Marie: You shut up!

Mary J: Or what?

Marie: Or else.

Mary J: You're going to batter me with your gammy hand?

Marie throws a slap at Mary J who ducks and runs around her. Marie sits and starts tying the bandages.

Mary J sits beside her.

Mary J: That doesn't fool anybody. Everybody knows yer back making rosary beads.

Marie: Shut up.

Marie continues wrapping the bandages around her fingers, Mary J observes this with exaggerated interest.

Children's voices are heard at the top of the stairs. Mary J and Marie listen.

Edel: *[Off]* Ok. There's nobody here. is everybody ready?

Edel slowly emerges into the yard.

Mary J nudges Marie.

Mary J: Let's hide. Go on, we're invisible.

Mary J and Marie hide in the shadows.

Edel: Come on.

Anne emerges into the yard.

Anne: I'm ready. Bernadette?

Bernadette and Mary L appear.

Mary L: Last one.

Bernadette: Are ye sure this is gonna work?

Edel: It'll be fine. Just act normal.

Mary L: How dja act normal?

Edel: Just act stupid normal.

Bernadette: Stupid normal?

Edel: *[Sighs]* Just go to the fence – you've all got tea towels for the barbed wire?

The other three children nod affirmatively.

Bernadette: I'm scared.

Mary L: I'm shitting meself.

Pause.

Edel: Look let's just head straight to the back entrance of the school and head off. This is it.

Anne: This is it.

Edel: It's now or never. We're going. We're going to the outside world.

Bernadette: The outside world.

Edel: The outside.

Mary L: I'm really shitting meself.

Anne: Really?

Mary L: Nooooo.

Edel: We just go through the main gates and we're in Keogh Square. And once we're out we're out! Look go left and left again that'll confuse them because all cars drive on the right. Then we make our way to Lough Conn Road. That's where Anne's auntie lives.

Bernadette: And she knows were coming?

Anne: She'll know when we get there.

Mary L: Oh god! I'm s-

Anne, Edel & Bernadette: Shush!!!

Edel: Come on. Let's go!

Anne: Lough Conn Road! Ballyfermot here we come!

Exit Anne, Edel, Bernadette and Mary L.

Mary J and Marie emerge from the shadows.

Mary J: They're not going anywhere.

Marie: Why not?

Mary J: Cause we are going to tell on them.

Marie: We will not.

Mary J: We will so.

Marie: No, we won't.

Mary J: We'll get sweets.

Pause.

Mary J: If we wait till they've actually escaped, we might even get ice cream.

Marie: Ice cream?

Mary J: Yeah, and besides what have them brats ever done for us.

Marie: Edel broke me fingers. I didn't have to make rosary beads. There's no way I'm going to stick a knife in her back. We're not saying a word.

Mary J: Ice cream.

Marie grabs Mary J.

Marie: Don't say an effing word or I will batter you. Do you hear me?

Mary J: Jaysus yeah. Marie. I'll say nothing. Cross me heart and hope one day they'll give me a pie.

Marie: Not an effing word.

Mary J: My lips are sealed. Let's go into the dance.

Blackout. Traditional Irish music fades away.

Fade up.

Streetlights.

Anne, Edel and Bernadette appear walking slowly and looking weary and shivering.

Anne: Were lost. We have to ask somebody where Hong Kong road is.

Edel: We can't risk it.

Bernadette: We've been going round in circles. Were at Emmet Road again.

Anne: This turn left and keep on turning left plan isn't really working. We're still in Inchicore.

Bernadette: We'll never make it to Ballyfermot. I'll never see Hong Kong road.

Anne: We have to ask somebody.

Edel: We can't. We can't go back there. They'll murder us.

Pause.

The children look frightened and alone.

Anne: Look there's Orla Murphy.

Bernadette: Who's she?

Edel: She used to be in Goldenbridge. They let her out about a couple of years ago.

Bernadette: Could we ask her where Hong Kong road is?

Anne: Orla! Orla Murphy!

Edel: Shush!

A figure appears in the streetlight. It is a girl a few years older than the three children. She is very fashionably dressed with a trendy hair-do and is wearing red lipstick.

Orla: Who are yous? How do you know my name?

Anne: You're Orla Murphy. You were in Goldenbridge.

Edel: They let you out about two years ago.

Orla looks around suspiciously.

Orla: What are yous doing out so late? How come yer on yer own? What are you doing? Where are you going?

Pause.

Edel: We are escaping. We are going to stay with Anne's auntie. She has tomatoes.

Orla: And where is that?

Edel: Hong Kong road, Ballyfermot.

Orla: Hong Kong in Ballyfermot? Never heard of it. And how are you going to get there?

Edel: We are walking.

Orla: Ballyfermot's four or five miles. It'll take you ages. How long did it take you to get this far?

Anne: What time is it?

Orla checks her watch.

Orla: It's nearly nine o'clock, girls.

Anne: Well we left at sevenish …

Edel: We've been walking for two hours and were still only at Emmet Road.

The children start sobbing

Orla: Ye poor little girls.

Bernadette: It all went wrong from the start we shouldn't have left Mary L stuck in the barbed wire.

Orla: Who's Mary L?

Anne: She was part of the escape party.

Orla: And where is she?

Edel: She's stuck on the fence outside the church at Goldenbridge. We had to leave her. We have to get to Hong Kong Road.

Anne: Ballyfermot.

Bernadette: Will you take us there?

Orla smiles sympathetically.

Orla: Ah girls. It's not going to work. I can't take you to Ballyfermot. It's not safe after dark. You have to go back to the convent.

Anne/ Edel/ Bernadette: No, no, no! / Please!!! /We can't go back!!! /Sister Etrusca Lisieux will kill us!

Orla: Girls, look, yous have nowhere to sleep. It's past yer bedtime. Look. Shush. I'll bring yous back. I'll explain to the nuns that ye just wandered out and got lost. It'll all be fine. I can tell them you've never been on the outside on yer own. It will be fine. Everything will be fine in the morning. Come here give me a big hug girls.

The children huddle around Orla. Gently their sobbing subsides.

Orla: It's not too far. Let's all hold hands.

Bernadette: Could you be me mammy?

Orla: *[Laughs gently]* I'm too young to be yer mammy.

Bernadette: But yer all grown up.

Orla: In comparison to you maybe. I'm finding me feet in the world. I'm not ready to be a mammy.

Edel: I love your clothes, and your lipstick and your hair is only beautiful.

Orla: Thanks' love. I work in a hairdressers. The girls are brilliant with hair.

Anne: What's it like to work?

Orla: Ah it's fab. I have money to by nice clothes and things. The girls are fab, the customers are fab, I share a flat with three other girls. It's all great.

Edel: I'm going to be a hairdresser and have a lovely flat of me own.

Anne: I'm gonna have nice clothes and nice hair. I'm gonna have whatever hair-do I like.

Bernadette: I'm gonna get loads of ice cream.

Edel: I can't wait to get on the outside.

Orla: The outside's not easy either. For some young wans it's far worse than Goldenbridge.

Anne: Worse than Goldenbridge? That's mad.

Exeunt

Blackout

Lights fade up.

Orla, Anne, Edel and Bernadette are talking to Sister Etrusca Lisieux and a Lay Person.

Orla: The poor little things had never been in the outside world. They just wanted to have a look at the graveyard after dark but they got scared and they got lost. Isn't it lucky I found yous girls?

Anne, Edel *and* **Bernadette:** Thanks very much Miss Murphy.

Sister Etrusca Lisieux: You are very good Orla.

Orla: Thanks' Sister Etrusca Lisieux.

Sister Etrusca Lisieux: My little lost lambs. Look at you. Look at you. Thank you very much Orla. Don't be a stranger. Girls wave goodbye to Miss Murphy.

Anne, Edel *and* **Bernadette:** Goodbye Miss Murphy.

Exit Orla.

Anne, Edel and Bernadette Sister Etrusca Lisieux and the Lay Person all wave.

Sister Etrusca Lisieux: You ungrateful little brats.

Blackout.

ACT ONE

SCENE 9

Blank Canvas

Intertitle: **Blank Canvas**

A group of children, naked except for towels are huddled in the corridor. They are whispering nervously.

There is a press marked "SANITARY PRESS" beside a cracked mirror on the wall.

Bernadette: I thought we'd never make it to Hong Kong Road.

Edel: We'd been walking for hours. We had to stop and hide from the Guards – loads a times.

Anne: When all of a sudden, I see Orla Murphy.

Mary J, Marie and **Maggy:** Who's she?

Bernadette: Orla Murphy!?

Anne: You don't know who Orla Murphy is?

Impressed silence.

Edel: She used to be here.

Bernadette: She was number fifty-two.

Anne: We met her on Emmet Road.

Bernadette: That's just around the corner.

Edel: We had to double back to avoid the Guards and there were nuns patrolling in Inchicore.

Moira: In the name of Jaysus!

Maggy: So how did you meet Orla Murphy?

Pause.

Edel: I says, we need to review the plan. It was my plan that we would go left at every turn because cars – you all know- go on the right … when all of a sudden Anne says:

Anne: I spy with my sharp eyes a beautiful lady.

Edel: She was walking under the streetlights like a movie star.

Anne: So glamorous.

Bernadette: Her coat and her shoes-

Edel: And her hair – she had such a gorgeous hairdo.

Anne: And she said she has a man.

Mary J, Marie and **Maggy:** Uuuuuh!

Edel: And he says she's his Moth.

Mary J, Marie and **Maggy:** Uuuuuh!

Marie: What does Moth mean?

Edel: It means he's going to marry her.

Anne: I'm going to get a man as soon as I leave here so I can be a Moth too.

The door at the end of the corridor opens.

Geraldine: It's Fat & Slimy Mary! She's got the Scabies Bucket and the paint brush!

The children quickly and nervously line up facing the "forth wall". Lay People - Nicola and Fat & Slimy Mary enter. Nicola is carrying a large beef tomato. Fat & Slimy Mary is carrying a Bucket and a medium sized masonry paint brush. Fat & Slimy Mary goes to the "SANITARY PRESS" she opens a four-gallon plastic container and pours its viscous white contents into the bucket. Nicola casually places the tomato on the top shelf in the press.

Nicola: You all know that smell girls.

Fat & Slimy Mary: It's Scabies abolition time!

Nicola: Don't miss a bit.

Fat & Slimy Mary: Ye what?

Nicola: Don't miss a bit.

Fat & Slimy Mary: Ye what?

Nicola: Just get on with it Picasso.

The children cling to their towels as Fat & Slimy Mary paints their backs from head to heel in the white viscous liquid. It is a slow excruciating process. Nicola and Fat & Slimy Mary take cruel pleasure from the children's ordeal. When they reach the final child. Fat & Slimy Mary gets another plastic container and refills the bucket.

Nicola: Turn around girls!

Fat & Slimy Mary: Drop yer towels.

The children turn and drop their towels. Fat & Slimy Mary is even more forceful than when painting the children's backs particularly when painting their genitals.

41

Fat & Slimy Mary: Wait till we get to yer fried eggs.

Nicola grabs her chest.

As Nicola and Fat & Slimy Mary near the end of the line Sister Etrusca Lisieux enters. She slowly walks up and down the line slowly twirling her large rosary beads while inspecting the painting of the scabies ointment. When Fat & Slimy Mary finishes painting the children, they all cover themselves with the towels.

Sister Etrusca Lisieux: Now. I have you all here. You, you and you step forward.

Anne, Bernadette and Edel step forward.

Sister Etrusca Lisieux: Now children. The rest of you listen very carefully. These three…

Pause.

Sister Etrusca Lisieux: You know what they did.

She slowly paces down the line.

Sister Etrusca Lisieux: They … Hmmm?

Pause.

Sister Etrusca Lisieux: They ran away. They…

All Children *[except Anne, Bernadette and Edel]* They ran away Sister Etrusca Lisieux.

Mary J: They went to Hong Kong, so they did.

Silence.

Sister Etrusca Lisieux: Now. Did you bring back scabies from Hong Kong?

Bernadette starts sobbing.

Sister Etrusca Lisieux: Nicola! *[Clicks fingers]* Bring me the wooden hand brush.

The three children huddle together.

Sister Etrusca Lisieux: Face the wall.

The three children face the wall.

Sister Etrusca Lisieux: You won't run away again! You *[she smacks Edel on the back of her legs with the wooden hand brush]*. Wont *[she smacks Anne on the back of her legs with the wooden hand brush]*. Run *[she smacks Bernadette on the back of her legs with the wooden hand brush]*. Away *[she smacks Edel on the back of her legs with the wooden hand brush]*. Again.

Sister Etrusca Lisieux: Nicola!

Sister Etrusca Lisieux hands Nicola the wooden hand brush.

Nicola repeats the beating several times. Each time she strikes - all the children witnessing the punishment gasp. Bernadette and Anne are crying. Edel is shocked but resolute. This enrages Nicola who is breathing heavily from her exertions.

Sister Etrusca Lisieux: Now. Girls. All of you go off and get dressed.

She is seething.

Sister Etrusca Lisieux: Mary! Get me the scissors.

She points at Edel

Sister Etrusca Lisieux: You get back here. Now. I know you were the ringleader. And let this be a lesson to all of you.

She grabs Edel by her hair and starts cutting it short. She is rough and imprecise. Edel stares at the floor. Sister Etrusca Lisieux finishes and clicks her fingers. She indicates the hair on the ground.

Sister Etrusca Lisieux: Nicola. Finish up here. Everyone else go and finish your rosary beads.

All but Nicola and Edel exit. Nicola attempts to click her fingers and gives Edel a sweeping brush.

Nicola: Now you clean up this mess. And put the buckets back in the press.

Exit Nicola. Edel sweeps up the hair and puts it in the bin. She glances at the cracked mirror. She stops momentarily. She then gets the scabies container and places it in the Sanitary Press. She sees the tomato. She looks around happy that everything is in its place. She takes the tomato and carefully examines it with her fingers. She smells it. She looks around. She takes a sloppy bite of the tomato. She pauses confused by and savoring the tomatoes flavour. She then places the half-eaten tomato back on the shelf.

Pause.

She retrieves the tomato and devours it. She sighs contentedly.

She goes to the mirror. She admires her new shorn look. She smiles. She then exits turning out the light.

ACT ONE

SCENE 10

Dust Tea Party and the Apple

Intertitle: **Dust Tea Party and the Apple**

Sound of rainfall.

The convent is dark apart from disparate religious statues dimly lit by candles.

Fade up on banister. Two children are whispering. They slide down the banister to the corridor. Carefully, they move along the corridor to the moonlit larder.

Fade up on highest part of the stage. A child's table and chairs are in a cluttered attic. Raindrops are on the window pane. Edel is seated playing with an imaginary tea set

Edel: Would you like some tea, Sarah?

Pause.

Edel: You would. Ok.

She pours imaginary tea from the imaginary pot into her imaginary friend's cup.

Edel: Oops I spilled some. Let me clean that up.

Edel carefully cleans the table around 'Sarah'.

Edel: Now put on your napkin like this.

Edel tucks an imaginary napkin into the neckline of her dress.

Edel: Very good. We don't want to get anything on your lovely dress.

Fade down.

The children enter the larder. They open a large cupboard it is well stocked with various food supplies. There is a large basket of apples on the central shelf. The girls make folds in their nighties and place handfuls of apples into the folds.

Fade up on attic.

Edel: I must tell you about my new Lady and Man. They're lovely so they are.

Pause.

Edel: Oh, it's a gorgeous house. Its got a garden out the front and in the back. And they've got an apple tree and all.

Pause.

Edel: They're kind of bitter but they're bellicious.

Pause.

Edel: It's in Coolock so it is.

Pause.

Edel: It's Coolock. Cool – ock.

Pause.

Edel: It's very cool to live in Coolock.

Pause.

` *The dining room door opens. Three Lay People arrive in. They are drunk.*

Mrs. Rilley: You should have seen the arse on him.

Fat & Slimy Mary: And his fly was down.

Nicola: You should have lit up a cigarette and blown the smoke in his face.

Fade down.

Fade up to attic.

Edel: Cake?

Edel cuts two slices of imaginary cake.

Edel: Mmmmmm! I could live on chocolate cake. Oh you've got some on your napkin. Just brush it off like this.

Pause.

Edel: I don't know what Mr. Andrews does but he has a big motor car. Missus Andrews makes clothes all day. And I stand like a mannequin [*Edel stands*] and she fits them onto me. But I can't wear them here because they're too nice. Anyway Mrs. Andrews says I'd stand out like a proper princess.

Edel pirouettes and sits.

Fade down.

Fade up on the pantry.

The Three Lay People are seated and talking raucously. The children are hiding behind the fridge clutching the apple filled folds.

Fade up on attic.

Edel: They have grown up daughters, so they do. One of them lives at home with them and the other one lives in Spain.

Pause.

47

Edel: Yeah, wow, Spain! And she was in Coolock the last time I was there. She kept saying things in Spanish. I'm going to learn Spanish when I grow up.

Edel stands.

Edel: The rain in Spain falls plainly on the man.

Edel sits down earnestly.

Edel: I don't know. He must have done something really bold and they put him outside in the rain.

Edel stands and pirouettes.

Edel: It's a green dress to go with my green eyes.

Pause.

Edel: I'll get her to make you a blue dress to go with your blue eyes.

Fade down.

Fade up on pantry. The Lay People are disgruntled talking about what they must do in the morning. An apple slips from one of the children's nighties. It rolls slowly across the floor, stopping near the table.

Fade down.

A shaft of moonlight shines through the window illuminating the floating dust in the attic.

Edel: Look at all that sparkly dust.

Pause.

Edel: Really. Is it magic dust?

Pause.

Edel: Oh look you've got some sparkly dust in your lovely blond hair. Is there any in my lovely red hair?

Edel pats her shorn head.

Fade down.

Fade up on scullery.

Nicola: I think we have ghosts.

Nicola walks over to the apple and lifts it up. She walks to the fridge and places it inside.

Mrs. Rilley: Should you not put that in the cupboard?

Pause

Fat & Slimy Mary: Ah it's been on the floor, put in the scraps for the brats tomorrow.

The Lay People cackle.

Nicola: They'll probably think it's their birthday.

Mrs. Rilley: Turn out the light Nicola.

The Lay People leave. The children make their way back to the dormitory.

Blackout.

Fade up to attic.

Edel: They're going to adopt me. I'm sure of it, well I hope they do.

Pause.

Edel: Of course I will. I'll ask them to adopt you too. We can be sisters. Together forever.

Edel hugs Sarah.

Fade.

ACT TWO

SCENE 1

Mizing

Intertitle: **Mizing**

Darkness.

A sash window opens.

Nicola rings a bell.

Nicola: Come and get it ye little savages.

Nicola and Fat & Slimy Mary empty a large tin basin of scraps from the window.

Sound of the children, they are fighting for scraps.

Fade up.

The children retreat to various parts of the yard selfishly holding onto the scraps of bread they have captured.

Edel, Mary J and Anne sit on the low wall. The other children also sit around the yard.

The children start eating their scraps. They soon slow down nibbling smaller and smaller pieces until the nibbles become minute.

They are looking at each other. They cautiously nibble at the edges of the bread. Each one is making a show of savouring the moment.

It is evident that all of the children wish to be the last one to finish the bread.

Mary J stands and turns her back on Edel and Anne. She breaks the bread and hides a portion up her sleeve. Anne stands beside Mary J. They both hold their bread preciously. Edel stops nibbling her bread holding it against her lips.

Edel stands forming a triangle with the other two.

Mary J takes a larger bite, Edel and Anne do likewise.

They warily regard each other. The watchful nibbling resumes. It slowly becomes evident that Mary J is not chewing.

Edel looks at her bread worriedly.

The three children continue nibbling for some time. When they are down to the last tiny morsel, they each stop.

The three stare at each other. Eventually Mary J holds her last morsel aloft. Suddenly she puts it in her mouth and swallows. She sits.

Edel puts her last morsel to her lips. Anne smiles and does the same. They both smirk at Mary J and swallow their last morsels simultaneously.

Edel sighs contentedly. Anne sits beside Mary J.

All of the children in the yard have finished their scraps.

Mary J stands on the wall. She grins slyly. With a triumphant flourish she removes the bread from her sleeve and scoffs it making a big show of swallowing.

Mary J retrieves the morsel from her mouth and holds it out between the two girls.

Edel puts her hand in her pocket. Mary J looks at her quizzically. Edel slowly takes her hand from her pocket and raises it to Mary J and deliberately opens her hand revealing a penny.

Mary J carefully takes the penny and examines it. Suddenly she puts the penny in her pocket and greedily devours the last morsel. She raises her arms in triumph.

Fade.

ACT TWO

SCENE 2

Seven Days in the Scullery

Intertitle: **Seven Days in the Scullery**

The children are seated making rosary beads. They are rocking rhythmically and counting.

The Angelus bell rings. The children stand in prayer.

The bell stops. The children resume their rosary bead making.

Enter Nicola. She walks up and down the line. She stops behind Edel. The children all glance at Edel who looks traumatized.

Nicola grabs Edel by the ears and hauls her to her feet. She turns Edel around holding her head, their faces are almost touching.

Nicola: You. Number Two. You're with me this week.

Pause.

Nicola: A whole week. Seven days.

Pause.

Nicola looks around and then violently slaps Edel across the back of her hands.

Nicola: What are you doing standing here? Don't stop making the rosary beads. You are in the Scullery for the whole week!

Silence.

Edel resumes making rosary beads. She starts counting. The other children join in the counting.

Exit Nicola.

[Off] **Nicola**: You are mine for a week! A whole week!

Edel: Jesus, Mary and Joseph.

Anne: Scrawny bitch.

Pause

Mary J: Think of the food you can rob.

Bernadette: The foods great in the scullery. That's where they make the Nun's food.

Anne: Could you get me a banana?

Edel: I'll try. If effing Nicola takes her eyes off of me.

Mart J: She'll batter ye all the same though.

Pause.

Anne: I'd love a tomato.

Bernadette: What's that?

Edel: It's red and it's roundy. It tastes amazing.

Pause

Mary J: The nuns get meat. Juicy meat.

Anne: We get cabbage stalks, lumpy potatoes and tapioca.

Bernadette: They get green leaves. Beautiful ones, not like the leaves in the field out the back.

Edel: The sour leaves. They're not the worst.

Anne: I totally agreen!

The children laugh.

Edel: A week in the scullery.

Pause.

Bernadette: No tapioca for them.

Anne: Boiled eggs. They get boiled eggs.

Mary J: Did ye hear what Nicola did to Moira with the gammy ears and the smell? She had to swally ten tablets of Cod liver oidl every day.

Bernadette: Ten tablets!

Anne: Every day!?

Edel: What would that do to you?

Mary J: It makes you shite. You shite till you can't stop. That … is why she has the poxy smell around her.

All the children stop making rosary beads.

A bell rings.

Bernadette: One, two, three, four –

All of the children resume making rosary beads and counting.

Anne: Good luck Siobhan.

Edel: Thanks, Anne.

Blackout.

Intertitle: **Day One**

The Kitchen. It is an industrial kitchen.

Enter Nicola and Edel. Nicola is holding Edel's hair. She leads the child to a row of very large pots.

Nicola: Now ye little wagon. Pots. Do you see them pots?

Edel: I do.

Nicola: The ones there in front of you.

Nicola pulls Edel's hair.

Nicola: Do you see them?

Edel: Yeah, I do see them.

Nicola: You do see them - what?

Nicola tugs Edel's hair.

Edel: I do see them - Nicola.

Nicola: Are they shiny or not shiny?

Edel: They are kind of shiny.

Nicola slaps Edel on the back of her head. She grabs a pot and puts it over Edel's head.

Nicola: Are they shiny or not shiny?

Edel: I don't know.

Nicola smacks the pot.

Nicola: The pots in my kitchen – my kitchen - are always shiny. You are my little bitch and you will make sure my pots are always shiny.

Pause.

Nicola: Are you listing to me Number Two? Hah?

Edel: I am.

Nicola: Now I want you to shine up all me pots.

Pause.

Nicola: What are you waiting on?

Edel: Can I take this pot off me head?

Nicola: Can you take the pot of yer head? Ye what? Hah?

Nicola impatiently grabs the pot off Edel's head and slaps the child's face. Edel recoils but stands defiantly.

Nicola: I want them all shiny. I want to see me face in them. Hah? Get that wire brush and the bucket.

Nicola throws an apron at Edel. She dons it and starts cleaning the pots with the wire brush.

During a slow fade Nicola makes a big show of being exasperated by Edel's work, intermittently smacking the back of her head.

Fade out.

Intertitle: **Day Two**

Soundscape: Montage of the sounds of manual labour.

The acting style is exaggerated and speeded up.

The lighting flickers.

Edel is kept constantly busy by Nicola who is a cruel taskmaster. Edel is cleaning floors, setting tables, and serving Lay People.

Nicola is friendly and chatty with the other Lay People.

Anne and Bernadette intermittently appear at the hatch. Edel surreptitiously throws bananas and oranges to them.

Sister Etrusca Lisieux appears at the hatch and speaks to Nicola. Unbeknownst to them Edel has a butter knife and pretends to stab Nicola. Edel hides the knife. Nicola notices Edel and berates her.

Blackout.

Intertitle: **Day Three**

Nicola is standing. Edel scrubs the floor in ever expanding circles around her.

Nicola: This is my kitchen. It's spotless so it is. Look at you ye little-little scrubber.

Pause.

Nicola: Dark little-little sin of a fallen woman. Look at you. Crawling. Where you belong. Down there.

Pause.

Nicola: Look at you Number two. Ha ha ha ha ha ah ha ha ah ha! I'm brilliant! Look at me spotless floor.

Pause.

Nicola: There she goes. A moving sin. Spotty soul. Little brat. Enemy of Jesus. Forsaken of Mary.

Nicola empties a bucket of dirty water on the floor.

Nicola: Unworthy. Thinks she's smart. Sin. She's made of sin. Scrubber. Little-little scrubber.

Pause.

Nicola: Smart little - If it wasn't for me where would you be? Hah?

Pause.

Nicola: This is my kitchen. Spotless.

Pause.

Nicola: My pots are shiny. I have gorgeous pots.

Nicola grabs a pot and shoves it onto Edel's head. Edel continues scrubbing the floor.

Nicola: The apple doesn't fall far from the tree. Your slut of a mother would have scrubbed better than you. Don't you look at me. Ha ha! Ye can't! Can ye? Ha ha ha aha ha ha! Your head in a pot. My pot.

Nicola looks around scrutinizing.

Nicola: Do you hear me? Have you got your listening ears on? Hah? Over there. That way. Steady as ye go. Scrub, scrub, scrub.

Pause.

Nicola: I'm brilliant. This is my kitchen.

Pause.

Nicola: *[Sings]* Blindly blindly so and sos. Shagged it up with the farmer's wife. See how they run. Bladay blady da! Giddily diddly da.

Pause.

Nicola: You missed a bit! No, no, no, no, no! Over there behind you. Go over there ye little-little scamp. Yer a waste of space. There! No. The other way. Do you not know yer right from yer left? Holy Mary and Jaysus. How long do I have to do this for?

Fade to blackout

Intertitle: **Day Four**

Nicola is talking to a Lay Person at the hatch. Edel is eating leftover sausages from the Lay Person's meal. There is a half-eaten slice of cake on the table. Edel looks around. Nicola is talking at the hatch. Edel grabs the cake and shoves it in her apron pocket.

Edel clears the table. Nicola sits tapping her feet in agitation. Edel finishes her duties.

Edel goes to leave. Nicola grabs her arm.

Nicola: Number Two. You. You little wagon. Smart arse. Do you think I'm some sort of stupid eejit? Like, me? It's me. I'm me. Hah?

Pause

Nicola: You didn't put that bucket back? Did ye?

Nicola shoves Edel.

Nicola: Who tidies away the bucket?

Exit Edel.

Blackout.

Intertitle: **Day Five**

A bell rings. Edel is hard at work.

She has a significantly bruised and bloodied black eye.

She opens a box of bananas.

Nicola and Sister Etrusca Lisieux are counting boxes of rosary beads brought to them by children.

Fat & Slimy Mary places the boxes of Rosaries into a large box labeled "Rosary Beads Hand Crafted by the Sisters of Mercy, St Vincent's School, Goldenbridge."

Anne appears at the hatch. Edel throws a banana through the hatch. Anne catches it.

Edel clenches her fist in triumph.

Blackout

Intertitle: **Day Six**

Nicola: Do you call that pot clean?

Edel: I'm doing my best Nicola.

Nicola slaps Edel.

Nicola: Why do ye always call me Nicola?

Pause.

Nicola: Do you want to get a smack?

Edel: No.

Nicola: No - what?

Edel: No – Nicola.

Nicola: You asked for this.

Nicola repeatedly slaps Edel into a corner. Edel collapses onto the floor.

Nicola: I want you to call me Miss. You call all the other lay people Miss. Why not me? You little brat. M – I – S – S. Miss!

Nicola is kneeling on Edel repeatedly hitting her.

Nicola: Do you hear me Number Two? I am a Miss. M – I – S – S. I don't miss with me fists. What do you call me?

Edel: Miss.

Pause

Nicola: Good girl, Number Two. One for the road.

Nicola punches Edel.

Blackout.

Intertitle: **Day Seven**

Lights up.

Nicola: I didn't say a stool. I said a spoon.

Edel: I heard you wrong.

Nicola: Come here to me. You asked for this.

Nicola smacks Edel.

Nicola: What did you do?

Edel: I asked for this.

Nicola smacks Edel.

Nicola: You asked for this - what?

Edel: Miss.

Nicola smacks Edel.

Nicola: Did I ask for a stool or a spoon? Hah?

Pause.

Edel: Well, eh, you didn't ask … for … what I was thinking is you were to look for either of them. You never know where to start do you?

Nicola: Did I say a spoon or a stool?

Edel: I'm always looking at questions like … em … ways to answer them, you know?

Nicola smacks Edel.

Nicola: You don't have a clue you smart bitch. Do ye?

Edel: I dunno.

Nicola grabs Edel's nose.

Nicola: That's not the question I asked you. Is it? Hah? It's not like a quiz. Like when the Nuns do the quiz on St Brigid's day. I have read the Bible a hundred times. Why can't you understand the difference between me asking you to get me a spoon or a stool?

Edel: I really don't know.

Nicola: Do you think I should put yer head in a pot?

Silence.

Edel: Please no.

Nicola: Please no ... what?

Edel: Miss?

Nicola: Say that again.

Edel: Miss.

Nicola releases Edel's nose.

Nicola: Too little too late. I am going to mangle you. What's yer favorite pot? Hah? *[Sings]* If I had a hammer/ I'd slam it on a pot/ If I had a hammer ...

Blackout.

ACT TWO

SCENE 3

The Murder Monologues

*Intertitle: **The Murder Monologues***

Dormitory.

Three of the children are in bed illuminated by torches they take from under their pillows.

Anne: I'd kill her. I'd kill her slowly. I'd love to peel her skin off. Hung upside-down. Star shaped. Both arms hung out. Both legs hung out. Star shaped. She'd be naked. I want to kill her slowly.

Bernadette: Strangulation isn't good enough. Death isn't even good enough. We must start with the itch stuff. Shove it in her. Right in her. Inside her.

Edel: She drags me kicking and screaming by the hair. She tells me to stay there in the dark. Apparently, I was making too much noise. She appears like a witch. I am screaming. By the hair. Down the corridor. Nicola. On her broom.

Anne: She has no feet. Her soul farts.

Bernadette: I have only fear. I hope the devil visits her tonight.

Edel: Every night. I'm scared. I'm scared every night.

Anne: Benediction with bells and spiders and rats. Flay the witch alive. Crust her knickers with mouldy bread.

Bernadette: Cut her in half.

Edel: Feed her to the pigs.

Anne: Ah leave the little pigs alone. Shoot her.

Bernadette: That would be too quick.

Edel: You can't kill a witch.

Anne: Yes, you can. Burn her. I'm feeling evil. I want her death. Shrivel her mortal soul. I'd have her hung upside down. Split her in two from the privates down.

Bernadette: Scratch her eyes out with rosary bead wire.

Edel: Make Nicola eat them.

Anne: Both eyes.

Bernadette: Make her watch.

Edel: Humiliate us all the time. In front of everyone. Fried eggs. I'd fry her in lard.

Anne: Her own lard.

Bernadette: Her own fried eggs.

Edel: Get the Sister to say a thousand Hail Marys.

Anne: Make a thousand rosary beads.

Bernadette: Make her hands fall off. Hairy Mary full of disgrace, slap her around all around the place.

Edel: Put her on fire.

Anne: Douse her with holy water.

Bernadette: Put her on fire again.

Edel: Have all the kids in the wet the bed dormitory put her in a bath of pee.

Anne: Get loads of bags of pee. Throw them at the nuns.

Bernadette: Make them drink it.

Edel: Holy piss.

Anne: Smother her with a mantilla.

Bernadette: Too many holes in them

Edel: Every mantilla in Goldenbridge.

Anne: Glory be. Cut off her gee.

Bernadette: If you want to frighten a child, dress as a nun.

Edel: Mad crooked hats.

Anne: Black habits. Bad habits.

Bernadette: Bad habits make your soul black.

Edel: How can a child dress if they want to frighten a nun?

Anne: Calablavas. Just enough eyes to see. We've got to murder them.

Bernadette: All of them.

Edel: Burn them to cinders. Yeah.

Anne: Strangle them with rosary beads.

Bernadette: Step by step. Word by word.

Edel: Amen. Awomen.

Anne: Smash her head in with the porcelain dolls.

Bernadette: We can never play with the porcelain dolls.

Edel: Eat the sweets first.

Anne: Infest her with rats. Big ones. Manky ones.

Bernadette: Break her bones. All of them.

Edel: Start with the fingers. I can break fingers. I know that sound. It's a crunch and a snap all at once. I can see the fear in her eyes.

Anne: We've already made her eat them.

Bernadette: A spear through her belly. I can smell the rotten guts.

Anne, Bernadette and **Edel:** That's disgusting!!!

Edel: Ten decades, ten murdered.

Anne: Dead.

Bernadette: As a doorbell.

Edel: Never rings. Nobody comes. Straight to hell.

Anne: Mourning and weeping. Valley of ears. Lamb of chop.

Bernadette: Nobody listens. Eternal damnation.

Edel: Pray the Hail Mary for ever and ever and ever and ever.

Anne: Smother her in her bed with a pillow.

Bernadette: In her cubicle. Make room for the Holy Ghost.

Edel: I'd love to smack her in the face with a wet fish.

Anne: Put her in the potato peeling machine with the witch.

Bernadette: Make chips out of them.

Edel: Give the chips to the Milkman.

Anne: He'd take us home with him. So he would.

Bernadette: I want to have a home.

Edel: I want to kill Sister Etrusca Lisieux.

Anne: Her as well.

Bernadette: Me too.

Edel: Cut her tongue out.

Anne: Make her pray.

Bernadette: Shove rosary beads in her ears till they fill her brain and all her holy holes.

Anne: Holy Show.

Bernadette: Meet her maker, who must be a bigger witch.

Anne: I'd give them fleas, scabies and warts.

Bernadette: All witches have warts.

Edel: [*Sighs*] This is better than food.

Blackout.

ACT TWO

SCENE 4

Edel and the Big Brown Box

Intertitle: **Edel and the Big Brown Box**

The children are in the big fancy visitor's room. It has a swirly patterned carpet, armchairs and couches adorned with doilies. Dozens of small porcelain dolls line high shelves. The bars on the windows are obscured by flowery patterned curtains. There is a TV on a shelf. It is off.

Enter Fat & Slimy Mary with some of the children.

Fat & Slimy Mary: Sit down there and don't move.

The children sit squashed together on a couch. Exit Fat & Slimy Mary.

Pause.

Edel stands and goes cautiously to one of the shelves with the dolls. She stretches and strains but cannot reach the dolls. She sighs and returns to the other girls and slumps down on the couch.

Edel: I love being in the fancy room. I can't reach the dolls though. See that one there? I was allowed play with that when the last Lady and Man visited.

Anne: Did you eat the lollipop?

Edel: Straight away. I ate it fast before they could take it away from me.

Mary J and **Bernadette:** Yeah we did that too.

71

Mary J: Do you think they'll give us lollipops for the confirmation?

Anne: I'm so excited me Auntie's going to be there.

Bernadette: Yer Auntie's coming?

Anne: She's coming all the way from Lough Conn Road.

Bernadette: Where's that?

Anne: Ballyfermot.

Bernadette: Ballyfermot? Oh yeah! Wow. Dja hear that?

Edel: Hear what?

Bernadette: Anne's auntie is coming to the confirmation. From Ballyfermot.

Anne: Lough Conn Road.

Bernadette: Do you have anyone coming?

Edel: No. Do you?

Bernadette: No.

Pause.

Enter Fat & Slimy Mary she is carrying a large battered old brown cardboard box.

Enter Sister Etrusca Lisieux. The Children stand.

Pause.

Sister Etrusca Lisieux walks to the centre of the room.

Sister Etrusca Lisieux: Put down the box Mary.

Pause.

Sister Etrusca Lisieux: As you know your confirmation is happening next Sunday. Pentecost Sunday. You are all going to become Soldiers of Christ.

Anne: Does that mean we have to fight Sister?

Sister Etrusca Lisieux slaps Anne hard in the face. Anne sobs dryly.

Sister Etrusca Lisieux: Stop your whimpering child. So. We come to the matter at hand. See this box. It is a remarkable box.

Everyone stares at the box.

Sister Etrusca Lisieux: This box contains Confirmation outfits worn by former girls who passed through our august establishment. Some of them are at least thirty years old.

She pats the box.

Sister Etrusca Lisieux: Isn't that wonderful girls? You, number two. Come up to the box.

Edel approaches the box. Sister Etrusca Lisieux pulls out a rough woollen two-piece green outfit with a green wide brimmed net hat.

Sister Etrusca Lisieux: Green. That will match your red hair. Go over there and put that on. So. Next.

One by one the Sister beckons each child to the box. She hurriedly and in a somewhat flustered and increasingly impatient manner selects outfits and hats for each child. This goes on until each child has donned their outfit.

Sister Etrusca Lisieux: Line up children let me look at you.

The children form an untidy motley line. The outfits and hats are of different shapes, sizes and eras.

Edel's skirt is too big for her, she holds it up.

Sister Etrusca Lisieux: Mary, get a safety pin for the child and fix that.

Fat & Slimy Mary reaches into her apron and retrieves a safety pin. Starting with Edel she adjusts the outfits of each of the girls in the line with varying degrees of success.

Sister Etrusca Lisieux: So it's important you have your saints' name for Pentecost Sunday. Your Confirmation Day. So. You, have you got a name? No. You will be Marion. Good. Next.

Bernadette: Bridget, sister.

Sister Etrusca Lisieux: Good our patron saint. You? What cat got your tongue? You will be Anne.

Anne: I am Anne, Sister.

Sister Etrusca Lisieux: Do you want to see the back of my hand again? Oh for God sake. Take Theresa.

Pause.

Right Number Two. You're getting Mary.

Edel: I am Mary already, Sister.

Sister Etrusca Lisieux: You're Siobhan.

Edel: I'm Siobhan Mary, Sister.

Silence.

Sister Etrusca Lisieux: Have you got a saint's name ready?

Edel: Edel.

Sister Etrusca Lisieux: Where did you hear that?

Edel: In a holy book, Sister.

Sister Etrusca Lisieux: Edel it is then. Right, we're done. Mary, get the costumes and put them in the box for next Sunday. Pentecost Sunday.

Exit Sister Etrusca Lisieux.

Edel: I am Edel.

Fat & Slimy Mary: So, its Edel now, is it? In your fancy costume. The black girl wore that for her confirmation. She was another troublemaker, so she was.

The Children exit.

Fade.

ACT TWO

SCENE 5

Dr Dolittle

Intertitle: **Dr Dolittle**

Fade up.

Sister Etrusca Lisieux is holding Edel by the hand in the Visitors Room.

Sister Etrusca Lisieux: Now Siobhan, you were very well behaved today at the confirmation. You need to keep this up. A Lady and Man are going to take you out for the day.

Edel is clearly excited.

Sister Etrusca Lisieux: Don't fidget. You are representing the Sisters of Mercy. Here they come now.

Sister Etrusca Lisieux smiles and waves weakly.

Sister Etrusca Lisieux: Before you leave remember everything you say – *everything* - you say comes back.

Enter the Lady and the Man.

Sister Etrusca Lisieux: Mr and Mrs Nolan hello and welcome to St Vincent's, Sisters of Mercy, Goldenbridge.

Mr Nolan: Thank you Sister.

Mrs Nolan: This must be Siobhan.

Edel is happy but nervous.

Sister Etrusca Lisieux: Say hello Siobhan Mary Edel.

Edel: Hello Mr. Lady, Hello Mrs. Man.

The adults laugh.

Mrs Nolan: It's Mr and Mrs. Nolan.

Edel: Hello Mr and Mrs Nolan.

Sister Etrusca Lisieux passes Edel to the Nolans who each hold her hands.

Sister Etrusca Lisieux: Mr and Mrs. Nolan will take care of you for the day.

Mr. Nolan: We are going to take you to the pictures.

Sister Etrusca Lisieux: What are you going to see at the Picture House? Hmmmm?

Mrs. Nolan: Dr Dolittle, Sister.

Edel: Is that about a hospital?

Mrs. Nolan: No, no. It's about a man who can talk to animals.

Edel: A fella who can talk to animals? I'd love to talk to animals.

Exit Sister Etrusca Lisieux. Crossfade. Edel and the Nolans enter the cinema. Edel is holding a bag of popcorn. She takes off her confirmation hat and puts the bag of popcorn in it. The opening credits play the lights of the screen flicker on Edel. She waves her hand like a conductor to the title music.

Mr. and Mrs. Nolan: What name did you take for your confirmation?

Edel: Edel. Call me Edel.

Mr. and Mrs. Nolan: Edel. That's lovely.

Edel: Are youz going to be my new Mammy and Daddy?

Mr and Mrs. Nolan look at each other uncomfortably.

Mrs Nolan: What's your favourite animal Edel?

Edel: There's a lamb out in the back field called Bambi. I love Bambi. After this film I'm going to go and talk to Bambi. I'll have an awful lot to say about me confirmation and about the film and about you Mr and Mrs Nolan.

Crossfade.

Mr and Mrs Nolan return Edel to Goldenbridge. Edel is clutching a bag of sweets.

Sister Etrusca Lisieux: You're back! Thank you so much Mr and Mrs. Nolan.

Edel grabs Sister Etrusca Lisieux's arm, the Sister swats her hand away.

Edel: These are the best Lady and Man ever. Look they gave me a bag of sweets!

Sister Etrusca Lisieux: Number two – Siobhan Mary Edel make sure to leave the sweets with a member of staff in here in the workroom.

Edel: Yes, I will sister.

Sister Etrusca Lisieux: Thank you so much for the gift of the sweets. It's too late for number – the child – for her to have them this evening. Bye for now Mr and Mrs. Nolan.

Mrs. Nolan: God be with you sister.

Sister Etrusca Lisieux: God be with you Mr and Mrs. Nolan.

Exit Mr and Mrs. Nolan.

Enter Nicola and Fat & Slimy Mary.

Nicola: Give us the goody bag.

Edel hands over the bag which Nicola and Fat & Slimy Mary greedily examine.

Fat & Slimy Mary: Dolly mixtures!

Nicola: Liquorice I love liquorice!

Fat & Slimy Mary: Bullseyes!

Nicola: Sugar coated jellies.

Fat & Slimy Mary: Yummier!

Nicola: I'm going to stuff me face.

They take most sweets from the bag and place it on the shelf with other bags.

Nicola: You can have them tomorrow.

Fat & Slimy Mary: If you're good.

Blackout.

ACT TWO

SCENE 6

Assumptive On Me Birthday

Intertitle: **Assumptive On Me Birthday**

Ten Children are seated in the classroom. Enter Sister Claudine and Sister Etrusca Lisieux. The Children all stand.

Sister Etrusca Lisieux: Suigh síos leanaí.

The Children all sit. Sister Claudine places two ledgers on the teachers' desk.

Sister Claudine: Today is an important occasion. Now. For administrative purposes we celebrate all your birthdays on September the eighth which is the Nativity of the Blessed Virgin. This year all of you will be fifteen years old. Fifteen.

Sister Etrusca Lisieux: Fifteen.

Sister Claudine: Next year will be your last. From now on we will celebrate your birthday on your *actual* birthday. Now.

Sister Etrusca Lisieux: So. We will call your number, your name, your *actual* birthday and an important event in the life of the Church that has its anniversary on that day.

Pause.

Sister Etrusca Lisieux: So. When I call your name stand up until I tell you to sit down.

The nuns open the ledgers.

Sister Claudine: Number one

Sister Etrusca Lisieux: Anne with an "E".

Anne stands up.

Sister Etrusca Lisieux: October the first.

Sister Claudine: On October the first in the year 266 Pope Damascus the first was elected.

Sister Etrusca Lisieux: Sit down number one.

Anne sits down.

Sister Claudine: Number two.

Sister Etrusca Lisieux: Edel.

Edel stands.

Sister Etrusca Lisieux: August 15.

Sister Claudine: August 15 is the day –

Sister Etrusca Lisieux: Wait.

Pause.

Sister Etrusca Lisieux: That is a most momentous day. We'll do you last number two.

Edel sits.

Sister Etrusca Lisieux: Stand up. I did not tell you to sit.

Edel stands.

Sister Claudine: We'll come to you last, but not least. Now. Number three.

Mary J stands.

Sister Etrusca Lisieux: Mary J. November 13.

Sister Claudine: On this day in World War One Allied troops occupy Constantinople, the capital of the Ottoman Empire.

Sister Etrusca Lisieux: Why they didn't take it from the filthy heathens I will never know.

Sister Claudine: Sit down Mary J.

Mary J sits.

Sister Claudine: Number four.

Sister Etrusca Lisieux: Moira.

Moira stands up.

Sister Etrusca Lisieux: May the fourth.

Sister Claudine: In 1493 Pope Alexander VI divides the New World between Spain and Portugal along the line of Demarcation.

Sister Etrusca Lisieux: Sit.

Moira sits.

Sister Claudine: Number five.

Sister Etrusca Lisieux: Marian.

Marian stands up.

Sister Etrusca Lisieux: September 12.

Sister Claudine: On this day in 1112 St Fortinbras defends Norway from the Sami Pagans.

Sister Claudine nods. Marian sits.

Sister Claudine: Number six.

Sister Etrusca Lisieux: Maggy.

Maggy stands up.

Sister Etrusca Lisieux: April the first.

Sister Claudine: On April –

Sister Etrusca Lisieux: Wait! We'll give this one an ice cream.

Maggy: Oh yes!

The nuns exchange glances and smirk.

Sister Etrusca Lisieux: Sit down Maggy.

Maggy sits.

Sister Claudine: Number Seven.

Sister Etrusca Lisieux: Marie.

Marie stands up.

Sister Etrusca Lisieux: December 21.

Sister Claudine: The feast of St Honoratus of Toulouse.

Sister Claudine nods. Marie sits.

Sister Claudine: Number Eight.

Sister Etrusca Lisieux: Bernadette.

Bernadette stands up.

Sister Etrusca Lisieux: September 22.

Sister Claudine: The last hanging of those convicted of witchcraft in the Salem Witch trials.

Sister Etrusca Lisieux: Bernadette! Are you a little witch?

Sister Claudine: I would be most upset if I looked in your soul and saw a witch in there!

Sister Etrusca Lisieux: Very upset!

Bernadette looks extremely frightened and is on the verge of tears.

Sister Etrusca Lisieux: Oh, sit down. This is supposed to be a day of joy.

Bernadette sits down sadly.

Sister Etrusca Lisieux: Now. Sister Claudine tell Nicola to bring the girls some lollipops. You would like a lollipop girls?

All Children: Yes please! Sister Etrusca Lisieux!

Sister Claudine opens the classroom door.

Sister Claudine: Nicola!

[Off] **Nicola:** *[Loud indistinguishable reply].*

Sister Claudine: Bring ten lollipops to the classroom!

[Off] **Nicola:** *[Loud indistinguishable reply].*

Sister Claudine returns to the desk

Sister Claudine: Now. Number Nine.

Sister Etrusca Lisieux: Mary L.

Mary L stands up.

Sister Etrusca Lisieux: October 4.

Sister Claudine: 1582. The Gregorian calendar is introduced by Pope Gregory XIII. That's how we know when your birthday is. Calendars and chronologies are most excellent things.

Sister Etrusca Lisieux: So. Finally.

Sister Claudine: Number ten.

Edel: Sister, I …

Sister Etrusca Lisieux: Do you have something to say?

Edel: *[Very quietly]* No Sister Etrusca Lisieux.

Sister Claudine: Edel, child. Good things come to those who wait.

Sister Etrusca Lisieux: So. Wait.

Sister Claudine: Now. Number ten.

Sister Etrusca Lisieux: Geraldine.

` *Geraldine stands up.*

Sister Etrusca Lisieux: June 22.

Sister Claudine: 1633 – The Holy Office in Rome forces Galileo Galilei to recant his view that the Sun, not the Earth, is the center of the Universe. This unfortunately was a mistake.

Sister Etrusca Lisieux: Indeed, Sister Claudine. Priests aren't always right but Nuns are. So. Children. Nuns are always …

Sister Claudine: Nuns are always … Right. Nuns are always …

All Children: Right.

Edel softly coughs.

Sister Claudine: Oh yes. Now Edel. August 15 a most especial day! A glorious day in the history of the One True Church.

Sister Etrusca Lisieux: August 15 is the day the most Holy Blessed Virgin was embraced by the hordes of angels and Ascended up into Heaven.

Sister Claudine: The Assumption of Mary into Heaven!

Sister Etrusca Lisieux: Child do you understand the significance of having such an important Birthday?

Sister Claudine: Do you, Edel? Do you understand?

Sister Etrusca Lisieux: It is the day of the feast of the Assumption of our Lady into in heaven!

Edel raises her hands. She hears Angelic music. She is bathed in Heavenly light.

Nicola enters the room and yells "scraps!" as she throws a shower of lollipops in the air.

Oblivious, Edel climbs onto the desk.

The Children scramble and fight for the lollipops. Sister Claudine tries to separate them and falls over.

Sister Etrusca Lisieux berates Nicola. They fade as Edel glories in the angelic light and music.

Edel: I am the chosen one. I am Assumpted into Heaven! Our Lady has given me miracles'. There will be loaves and there will be fishes. I will give bread to all the children. Rosary beads will make themselves. I will bury all the Nuns canes so the children will not be hit with them. I will bury the canes in the field out the back. The Nuns will spank the Lay People and the Children will beat the Nuns. There will be Ice Cream and Apples. There will be tomatoes for everyone! We will have nice clothes. We will have clean clothes. I will make the fleas vanish. I will remove the slime from the fish tank. I will make the fish tank clean!

Pause.

Edel: Thank you our Lady. I am here for you! I am here for us all! I am the Assumpted One!

The angelic music swells all light fades until only Edel's upturned and ecstatic face is lit.

Fade.

ACT TWO

SCENE 7

Dead Fish

Intertitle: **Dead Fish**

A group of children are standing in a line. There is a strong sense of apprehension. A Nun is standing opposite.

Sister Claudine: Children we all know why you are here. Sometime yesterday afternoon someone – one of you – let all of the water out of the fish tank. The fish are dead. All of them. And there are puddles of water all over the landing floor. One of you is going to clean it all up. The rest of you will stand – on one foot only -with your hands by your sides until the task is done.

Pause.

Sister Claudine: Which one of you did the deed?

Sister Claudine walks the line inspecting each of the children.

Sister Claudine: I have studied criminology. Theological criminology. The wisdom of Socrates. The forensic artifice of St Thomas Aquinas. The guile and moral rectitude of St Fortinbras the steadfast. Oh yes. I have studied them all.

Pause.

Sister Claudine: And do you know what that means? Do you? Well, do you? Hmmm?

Pause.

Sister Claudine: I can see your souls. I am a Bride of Christ.

The children all cover their chests with their hands hastily putting their hands together in prayer.

Sister Claudine: Your very souls. Your mortal souls. Your very mortal souls and I can see your sins. I can see your mortal sins!

The children all speak at once in a panicked cacophony of denial.

Sister Claudine: Quiet please. Tut tut. Children. Be quiet. Be calm. I ... can ... see ... your ... sins.

Some of the children scream. Some of the children pray with silent intensity ... Mary L prays out loud.

Mary L: Matthew, Mark and Luke and John/ God bless this bed that I lie on/ Four corners around my bed/ and four angels over my head/ If I be dead or die of sleep/ I'll give her my soul for her to keep.

Sister Claudine walks up and down the line of children with a pointed hand outstretched, divining. She stops at Edel.

Sister Claudine: Did you do it?

Edel: No Sister.

Sister Claudine: Do you know who did it?

Edel: No Sister.

Pause.

Sister Claudine: Right! All of you stand on one leg! Now!

The frightened children attempt to stand on one leg, most of them fall to the floor.

Sister Claudine: Oh Lord…Give me patience. All of you stand on two feet. I have patience.

Sister Claudine walks up and down the line. She stops at Bernadette.

Sister Claudine: Did you do it?

Bernadette: No sister.

She stops at Anne.

Sister Claudine: Did you do it?

Anne: No sister.

Sister Claudine: I don't suppose you did it, Mary L?

Mary L: No, I didn't sister!

Sister Claudine: And I would expect there's no point in asking you who killed the fish?

Mary L: I don't know sister.

Sister Claudine returns to the front of the line.

Sister Claudine: Right so. None of you are going to own up. Well in that case you must all be punished. None of you are going to the Disco! Hummph!

The children gasp in disappointment.

Blackout.

ACT TWO

SCENE 8

The End

*Intertitle: **The End***

Goldenbridge is quiet.

There is a light on in the office.

The Dormitory has been divided into cubicles.

The curtain swishes open in the first cubicle.

Enter Anne and Edel.

Edel: Welcome to my palace.

Anne: It's the same size as my cubicle.

Edel: But it's all mine. Look I got me ornament and me Mickey Mouse toothbrush on me dresser.

Anne grabs Edel's arm and points at the wall.

Anne: Jaysus. That's Donny Osmond! Where did ye get that?

Edel: A Lady and a Man.

Anne: They're a great Lady and Man.

Edel is quiet. She sits on the bed.

Edel: And they called it ... Ready? 1, 2 -3!

Anne and **Edel:** *[Singing]* And they called it puppy love

Oh I guess they'll never know

How a young heart really feels

And why I love her so!

Enter Mary J.

Mary J: What's going on?

Anne: Edel's got a Donny Osmond poster. Look!

Mary J: Yummy.

Pause.

Anne: What's up with you?

Mary J: I'm looking for Bernadette.

Edel: She's gone. Everybody's leaving. There's hardly any new young wans.

Mary J: Bernadette's gone gone?

Anne: Yeah, she left last week. Her and Johnny Thing and Mad Mad Mary all left the same day.

Edel: Why did they call her Johnny Thing?

Anne and **Mary J:** Because she walks like a fella.

A bell rings.

Mary J: Effing rosary beads.

In the Kitchen Mrs Rilley is admonishing Mary L who is struggling to return a large pot to its shelf. Pots crash to the floor

A bell rings.

The Rosary Bead room.

Sister Claudine, Ann, Edel, Mary J and **Geraldine:** To thee do we cry, poor banished children of Eve, to thee do we send up our sighs, mourning and weeping in this valley of tears. Turn, then, most gracious advocate, thine eyes of mercy toward us; and after this our exile show unto us the blessed fruit of thy womb Jesus.

Amen.

All bless themselves.

Sister Claudine: Right so. Children. One!

Children: Two, three, four, five, six,

Sister Claudine: Seven –eight –nine-ten!!! Work faster we must make the quota.

Mary J: There's only four of us.

Sister Claudine slaps Mary J's face.

Sister Claudine: You are paying for the sins of your slut mother. Work faster!

The children count and make beads. Their counting is rapid.

Sister Claudine: That's better.

Exit Sister Claudine.

Mary J: *[Sobbing]* Jesus Mary and shite.

Edel: I want to kill her.

Anne: Fleas, scabies and warts.

Geraldine: She can't smile.

Edel: How dja mean?

Geraldine: If she smiled her face would break.

Anne, Edel and Geraldine laugh.

Mary J: Shush! That witch can hear the grass grow.

Enter Mary L.

Anne: Where were you?

Mary L: I was in the kitchen. I had to do the pots.

Mary J: We've had to do the beads.

Edel: Leave it out Mary J.

Mary L joins in the rosary bead making.

Mary L: Wait till I tell yiz. I have news.

Mary J: What news?

Mary L: I was in the kitchen right –

Mary J: We know you were in the kitchen.

Edel: Tell us your news.

Mary L: Nicola has left Goldenbridge!!!

Anne/Edel/Geraldine/Mary J: What!!!/Jaysus!!!/Gone to hell!!! How do you know?

Edel: Mary how do you know?

Mary L: Miss Rilley told me.

Anne/Edel/Geraldine/Mary J: Dja believe her? / When did she go?/ What did Mrs Rilley Say?/ Where'd she go?

Mary L: Miss Rilley said so. I swear … she's gone

The children all cheer and hug.

All: *[Singing]* Ding dong the witch is dead!

Which old witch?

The wicked witch!

Ding dong the wicked witch is dead!!!

Edel slips away from the group. She takes a pliers from the table and runs to the kitchen. A radio is playing pop music. Mrs Rilley is there looking in a mirror and removing her nasal hairs with a tweezers.

Edel: Mrs Rilley, Miss.

Pause.

Mrs. Rilley: What are you doing here Number Two?

Edel: I'm looking for Nicola.

Mrs. Rilley: And why would ye be wanting to do that?

Edel: She asked me to get the long pliers, Miss.

Mrs. Rilley: What for?

Edel: To fix the gammy pot.

Mrs. Rilley: The gammy pot?

Edel: On the shelf … one of them … Nicola knows which one.

Mrs. Rilley: She's gone, so she is.

Edel: She's gone?

Mrs. Rilley: Left me in charge of the kitchen, so she did. She didn't say anything about a gammy pot.

Edel: Where's she gone, Mrs. Rilley?

Mrs. Rilley: She's gone to America. Her cousin got her a job working in a crèche. That's so cushy for her she'll be looking after toddlers instead of you brats.

Edel: When did she go?

Mrs. Rilley: Yesterday. I'm in charge now, so I am.

Pause.

Edel hands Mrs. Rilley the pliers. Mrs. Rilley is now holding both the tweezers and pliers. Edel runs back out of the kitchen.

Blackout.

Fade up.

Anne and Edel are at the top of the bannisters. They are whispering. Edel tucks up her nighty and slides down the bannisters. Doing likewise Anne follows.

Cautiously they enter the kitchen. Edel turns the light switch on.

They gasp. There is no one there.

Slowly at first, they adventure around the kitchen. Edel opens a fridge and gorges on tomatoes.

Anne builds a pyramid out of the pots. She gently taps out a tune with her fingertips on the pyramid.

The girls tiptoe away. Edel turns out the light switch. The fridge is open and untidy, its light illuminates the pyramid of pots.

Fade.

A bell rings.

Fade up.

Anne and Edel are descending the balcony steps singing.

Anne and Edel: *[Singing]* We're gonna get hi hi hi

The night is young

She'll be my funky little mama

Gonna rock it and we've only just begun!

Sister Etrusca Lisieux is standing at the bottom of the stairs.

Sister Etrusca Lisieux: Cunas! Where did you learn that obscenity?

Edel: It's Paul McCartney and the Beatles, sister. It's on the radio in the kitchen.

Anne: Mrs. Rilley likes it, sister. She's always singing the bit about the banana: "Sweet banana, you've never been done/ Yes, I go like a rabbit, gonna grab it"

Sister Etrusca Lisieux slaps Anne's face.

Sister Etrusca Lisieux: Off with you. There are rosary beads to be made. There's a quota to be met.

The girls move to depart. Sister Etrusca Lisieux grabs Edel's arm. Exit Anne.

Sister Etrusca Lisieux: Siobhan what date is it today?

Edel: Friday.

Sister Etrusca Lisieux: Date. Not day. I said date. What date is it today?

Edel: It's the tenth.

Sister Etrusca Lisieux: And next week on the fifteenth – the date of the Assumption of our Lady – is your birthday. Your sixteenth birthday. A very significant birthday. Do you know what that means?

Edel: Cake? Tea and Biscuits?

Sister Etrusca Lisieux: Tut-tut. It means you are leaving.

Edel: Leaving? Leaving where?

Sister Etrusca Lisieux: Here.

Pause.

Sister Etrusca Lisieux: The Sisters of Mercy, St Vincent's Industrial School, Goldenbridge.

Edel: Why?

Sister Etrusca Lisieux: Lord give me patience. Next Wednesday you are sixteen and when you are sixteen you must leave. There is no place for you here.

Edel: Where will I go?

Sister Etrusca Lisieux: You have relatives in Rialto. They can take you.

Edel: I don't know them very well.

Sister Etrusca Lisieux: That makes no difference.

Edel: But they smoke.

Sister Etrusca Lisieux: [*Exasperated*] Child.

Edel: They've got babies.

Sister Etrusca Lisieux: Perfect you can help with the babysitting. So that's next Wednesday … You had better prepare to pack your things.

Edel looks confused.

Sister Etrusca Lisieux: Not now. Off with you. The rosary beads won't make themselves.

Blackout.

Fade up.

Edel opens the door to her cubicle. She has a plastic shopping bag. She opens her dresser and removes a small number of neatly folded clothes and places them in her bag. She takes the Virgin Mary statue and the ornament from the dresser and puts them in her bag. She holds up the Mickey Mouse toothbrush. She looks at it lovingly before placing it back on the dresser.

Edel: Somebody else can have you, Mickey Mouse.

She carefully removes her Donny Osmond poster from the wall and loving rolls it up. She ties the poster in a green bow. She puts on her light coat and leaves the cubicle gently pulling the curtain closed.

At the top of the stairwell she touches the banister and looks around. She quickly descends the stairwell. She places her bag, poster and jacket at the bottom of the stairs.

She swiftly runs up to the top of the stairs. She mounts the banister and slides down it.

Edel: Geronimo!!!

Sister Etrusca Lisieux appears at the bottom of the stairwell.

Sister Etrusca Lisieux: Are you happy now?

Edel is embarrassed and clumsily gathers her belongings.

Edel: I'm all set.

Sister Etrusca Lisieux: God be with you, Go in peace, glorifying the lord by your life … Amen.

Pause

Sister Etrusca Lisieux: Amen.

Pause

Sister Etrusca Lisieux: Amen, Siobhan.

Pause

Edel: Call me Edel.

Sister Etrusca Lisieux: I beg your pardon?

Edel: It's the only name I chose. My mother called me Siobhan, but she was never in my life. I am Edel.

Pause

Sister Etrusca Lisieux: God be with you, Go in peace, glorifying the lord by your life … Amen.

Edel: Goodbye then, sister.

Edel walks away from Goldenbridge.

Sister Etrusca Lisieux: Child! Child! Siobhan! Edel!

Edel turns.

Sister Etrusca Lisieux: One last thing. If a man asks you to sit on his lap, make sure to put a newspaper between you.

Pause.

Edel: Herald or Press?

Sister Etrusca Lisieux: *[Sighs]* Off with you.

Edel turns and walks away.

She takes a deep breath.

Edel: Geronimo!

Blackout.

-The end-

APPENDICES

THE PLAY THAT WOULDN'T
GET LOCKED DOWN

On March 10th, 2020, the Doras Buí Drama Group met for a tour of Dublin's Abbey Theatre. Shortly after in a nearby hotel Susan Connolly and Cormac P. Walsh announced to the group that they had completed the first draft of *I Am Edel* as an eighteen-scene stage play. Two days later, Ireland entered into lockdown because of the Covid -19 pandemic. The government shut schools, childcare facilities and cultural institutions. For Connolly it was a dark day. With theatres closing she wondered if she could realise her dream of staging *I Am Edel* in its entirety.

The previous November Doras Buí staged three scenes from *I Am Edel* at Doras Buí in Coolock. These were, *I Could be Geronimo, Hong Kong* and *Assumptive on me Birthday*. This staging was filmed by Near TV and a short video of the event is available on line <u>I am Edel - Doras Buí Play - YouTube</u>.

This followed on from early drafts of scenes *Geronimo, Rosary Beads* and *Fatima in June 2019.* These had been workshopped with the Christine Buckley Centre Drama Group and with Colm Quearney of Fighting Words at Dublin University Players. These scenes and two songs written by Susan Connolly were performed at the Christine Buckley Centre.

Wishing to work with young actors to develop the eighteen scene first draft Connolly and Walsh made contact with Crooked House youth theatre in Connolly's hometown of Newbridge. The meeting scheduled for March 16 was cancelled due to the pandemic.

In the ensuing lockdown, work halted on the *I Am Edel* until June 2020 when Connolly and Walsh started exploring the possibility in adapting an abridged version of the play for radio. This was ultimately broadcast on July 6th, 2021 (details in the next appendix *The Radio Play*).

The eighteen-scene play is envisaged as a big production featuring nineteen characters performed by twelve actors on a set encompassing and recreating St Vincents Industrial School Goldenbridge. With the covid restrictions continuing into Autumn 2021, achieving staging of *I Am Edel* in its entirety seemed unlikely. The possibility of staging the abridged ten scene version with excerpts from *Seven Days in the Scullery* in a minimal black box setting was explored at this time.

Ultimately, Connolly and Walsh decided on the bold move of publishing *I Am Edel* in readiness for a post pandemic world.

THE RADIO PLAY

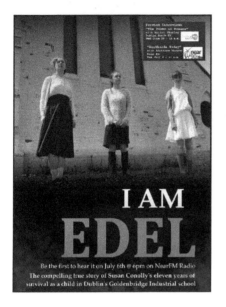

The radio play was broadcast on Near FM July 6th 2021 at 6 p.m. with the following introduction:

Introduction

I Am Edel by Susan Conolly and Cormac P. Walsh is an independent production put together by a diverse number of people in a diverse number of locations in Dublin and Kildare during the Covid -19 pandemic. It is a new Irish play with an all-female cast.

I Am Edel is a true story set in Dublin's notorious Goldenbridge Industrial school in the 1960's and 70's. Based on Susan Connolly's life in Goldenbridge. It is told from the perspective of a child from five to sixteen years of age. It reveals just what Susan and the other girls had to do to survive the harsh regime in an unforgiving world of Nuns and Lay people.

We are very thankful to Near FM for giving us the opportunity to air *I Am Edel*.

Working on zoom with the Christine Buckley Centre Drama Group and the Doras Bui Drama Group, Susan and Cormac adapted I Am Edel into the ten-scene radio play.

The script required actors with accent and age-appropriate voices. In the radio play the voices were provided by young people from Rialto Youth Project and Dublin youth theatre. In all there are ten voices recorded in ten different locations and mixed into a 53-minute Radio Play.

Cast

Note the radio play was originally developed on Zoom readings with members of Dublin Youth Theare and Rialto Youth Project: Aoife Connolly O'Sullivan, Charley Stephenson, Ciara Cochrane, Jennifer Davey, Kelsey Redmond, Robin Maher Kavanagh and Sophie Kerfoot.

Ciara Cochrane - Edel
Aoife Connolly O'Sullivan – Sister Etrusca Lisieux, Orla Murphy and Anne
Charley Stephenson – Fat N Slimy Mary *and* Maisey
Jennifer Davey – Children *and* Lay People
Kelsey Redmond - Children *and* Lay People
Rebecca Jordan – Children *and* Mary J
Robin Maher Kavanagh - Sister Claudine *and* Mary L
Sophie Kerfoot – Bernadette *and* Nicola
Susan Connolly – Children, Ann *and* Miss Rilley
Trudy Gorman – Nun's and Lay people

Production

Produced by Susan Connolly and Cormac Plunkett Walsh

Directed by the Cast

Edited by Cormac Plunkett Walsh for Radio Lockdown Productions

Graphic Design by Rebecca Jordan

Thanks to

The Christine Buckley Centre for Education and Support, Doras Bui, City of Dublin Education Training Board, Rialto Youth Project and Near FM.

This project was helped along the way by

Angie Gough, Carmel McDonell Byrne, Ciaran Colley, Dorothee Meyer-Holtkamp, Eddie Sherlock, Emilie Pine, Rhona Dunnet and Trudie Gorman.

Sponsored by Crafts by SE

I Am Edel *abridged for radio*

1. **The Beginning**
2. **How to Make Rosary Beads**
3. **I Could be Geronimo**
4. **Thank You**
5. **Mr. Patchy Britches**
6. **Hong Kong**
7. **Dust Tea Party**
8. **The Murder Monologues**
9. **Assumptive On Me Birthday**
10. **The End**

Listen on Near FM <u>Search Results for "I Am Edel" – Near FM – Listen Again</u>

DRAWINGS

"It takes many, many, many years of being on the outside of Goldenbridge before you realise what you went through in Goldenbridge."
Susan Connolly University College Dublin, National Folklore Collection Archive 4.10.2021.

During the process of writing *I Am Edel* Susan Connolly made a series of eyewitness drawings linked to scenes from the play.

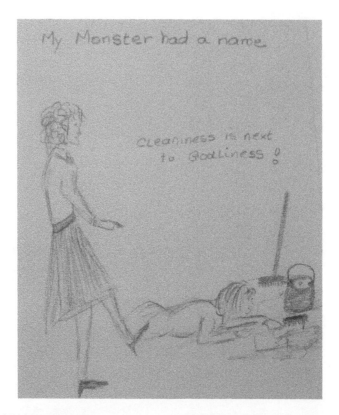

ABOUT THE AUTHORS

Susan Connolly is a remarkable storyteller and survivor of institutional abuse. She lives in Newbridge Co. Kildare. *I Am Edel* is her first published play. She is currently writing her autobiography *The Decades of My Life*.

Cormac P. Walsh is a drama tutor living and working in Dublin. His first novel *Serendipitous Fish* was Published in 2021.

ACKNOWLEDGEMENTS

Thanks to Christine Buckley Centre for Education and Support, Doras Bui, Dublin South FM Power of Dreams, KFM, Near FM and Rialto Youth Project

Carmel McDonnell Byrne, Clem Ryan, Cli Buckley, Críostóir MacCáthaigh, Emilie Pine, Marian Shanley and Martin Allioth.

Goldenbridge map from UCD History Hub.

COVER

Design by Rebecca Jordan

Photographed by Cormac P. Walsh

Featuring Ciara Cochrane, Aoife Connolly O'Sullivan and Robin Maher Kavanagh.

DEDICATION

This stage play is dedicated to my Goldenbridge sisters, brothers and my little runaway friends who are no longer with us.

-SC

Lightning Source UK Ltd.
Milton Keynes UK
UKHW010645180122
397331UK00001B/22